MW00791032

Days
of Praise®
FOR WOMEN

HARVEST HOUSE PUBLISHERS
EUGENE, OREGON

DAYS OF PRAISE is a registered trademark of Institute for Creation Research Corporation.

Scripture quotations are from the King James Version of the Bible.

Cover by Koechel Peterson & Associates Inc., Minneapolis, Minnesota

Cover photo © Hemera/Thinkstock

DAYS OF PRAISE® FOR WOMEN
Copyright © 2012 by Institute for Creation Research
Published by Harvest House Publishers
Eugene, Oregon 97402
www.harvesthousepublishers.com

ISBN 978-0-7369-4551-6 (pbk.)
ISBN 978-0-7369-4552-3 (eBook)

Printed in China

12 13 14 15 16 17 18 19 20 / FC-CD / 10 9 8 7 6 5 4 3 2 1

Introduction:

Giving Praise Every Day

*O how love I thy law! it is my
meditation all the day.*

Psalm 119:97

This devotional is designed to help you in your walk with the Lord each and every day so that you may understand God's Word more deeply and praise Him more passionately. We hope you will read each devotional thought along with the listed Scriptures to appreciate how deeply God wants to communicate His truth and love to you. As the Bible describes God's great program of redemption through the ages, it also features the individuals and relationships God has worked through to accomplish His marvelous plan.

Sprinkled throughout the Scriptures are moments of pleasure and pain, victory and defeat, faithfulness and failure, love and hatred, sternness and humor. God hides nothing about humanity; our challenge is to learn and apply the lessons He is teaching us through this marvelous Book.

We trust you will be encouraged to dig deeper into the written Word so you may walk more closely with Jesus Christ, the One who has been the Word from the very beginning.

Lawrence E. Ford
General Editor

Adam's Rib

And the rib, which the Lord God had
taken from man, made he a woman,
and brought her unto the man.

This amazing record of how the first woman came into being has been the object of much ridicule, but it is nonetheless true. The "rib" was most likely not a rib at all—the Hebrew word means either "side" or "side chamber."

It may be that God formed Eve's body from Adam's side or from something within the "chamber" of his side. The surgery must at least have involved the shedding of blood. "The life of the flesh is in the blood," so such a primeval blood transfusion from Adam's body would be uniquely appropriate to bring life to Eve's body.

Adam's "deep sleep" thus becomes a prophetic foreshadowing of "the last Adam," when a spear "pierced his side, and forthwith came there out blood and water." As Adam's sacrifice gave life to his bride, so did the death of Christ for "the church of God, which he hath purchased with his own blood." Just as Eve shared Adam's very life, so do believers today constitute Christ's beloved bride, and we are "hid with Christ in God," so that Christ Himself is "our life."

Scripture:

Genesis 2:21-22; Leviticus 17:11; 1 Corinthians 15:45;
John 19:34; Acts 20:28; Colossians 3:3-4

Disobedient Midwives

*The midwives feared God, and did not as
the king of Egypt commanded them.*

Shiphrah and Puah were midwives in Egypt who risked their
lives to prevent Pharaoh from murdering newborn males
among the Israelites. They courageously disobeyed and even
lied to Pharaoh. But Scripture says that "God dealt well with
the midwives." Bible critics frequently use this incident to
charge God with a tolerance of evil.

Two other women in the Bible, Tamar and Rahab, prosti-
tuted themselves but are direct ancestors of the Messiah. And
God even sent a "lying spirit" to do His bidding. So does God
actually "do evil, that good may come?" No!

"God cannot be tempted with evil," and it is "impossible for God to lie." God is absolutely holy and without any
"darkness at all." In the end, God will work "all things after the
counsel of his own will."

However difficult it may be to understand an apparent
conflict in circumstances, we must nonetheless "judge righteous judgment."

Scripture:
Exodus 1:17,20; Genesis 38:24; Joshua 6:25;
1 Kings 22:22-23; Romans 3:8; James 1:13; Hebrews 6:18;
1 John 1:5; Ephesians 1:11; John 7:24

Mary and the Grace of God

The angel said unto her, Fear not, Mary:
for thou hast found favor with God.

Gabriel's announcement to Mary that she had been chosen as the mother of the coming Savior contains the Bible's first use of *charis,* the Greek word for grace. Mary found grace with God.

In a remarkable Hebrew parallel, the first mention of grace in the Old Testament also heralds the coming of a new era: "But Noah found grace in the eyes of the LORD."

Grace is not something we earn; it is a treasure we find! But we find grace only because God's grace first finds us and reveals to us the Savior of our souls. Just as God found Moses in the desert and Paul on the road to Damascus, so He finds us.

Mary declared in her Magnificat, "My soul doth magnify the Lord, and my spirit hath rejoiced in God my Savior." This could well have been the testimony of Noah, and it surely should be the testimony of each of us who has found grace today.

Scripture:

Luke 1:30,46-47; Genesis 6:8

Mr. and Mrs. Adam

Male and female created he them; and blessed
them, and called their name Adam.

What is God's evaluation of the two sexes and their roles in His plan?

First, both man and woman were created in God's image, making them equal in salvation, rewards, and eternal fellowship with their Creator. "There is neither male nor female: for ye are all one in Christ Jesus."

At the same time, He named them both Adam, which is the proper generic word for the human race, as in "the LORD God formed man." When the woman was made from Adam's side, Adam said, "She shall be called Woman, because she was taken out of Man." This verse uses the Hebrew words *ish* for "man" and *isha* for "woman."

Also, Adam gave his new bride a personal name—Eve—because she was the "mother of all living."

God created man—both male and female human beings—in the beginning. Nevertheless, each of us has a distinctive personal name, and we can be thankful that God deals with each of us individually and expects us to individually fulfill the roles He has ordained for us.

Scripture:
Genesis 1:27; 2:7,23; 3:20; 5:2; Galatians 3:28

The Faith of Our Mothers

The unfeigned faith...dwelt first in thy
grandmother Lois, and thy mother Eunice.

Paul's "dearly beloved son" was a young disciple named Timothy, whose strong and sincere Christian faith was due to the lives and teachings of a godly mother and grandmother. "From a child thou hast known the holy scriptures."

Timothy's mother was a Christian Jew, but his father was an unbelieving Greek. Normally, the father is to assume spiritual leadership, but countless fathers are either unable or unwilling to do this. Many have been the homes where a mother or grandmother has had to assume this responsibility, and the Christian world owes these godly women a great debt of gratitude.

The fifth of God's Ten Commandments requires children to honor their parents, and it is the only one of the ten that carries a special promise: "That it may be well with thee, and thou mayest live long on the earth." Every godly parent is worthy of real honor every day—not just once each year. And when a Christian mother, like Timothy's mother, must assume all the responsibility for leading her children in the ways of God, she deserves very special praise.

Scripture:
2 Timothy 1:5; 3:15; Acts 16:1; Ephesians 5:22,25; 6:2-4

Lifelong Love

Live joyfully with the wife whom thou lovest.

King Solomon had 700 wives, all of whom were princesses. Most of these marriages were political unions, and Proverbs indicates that they did more harm than good. It is interesting that he had only one son, Rehoboam, and two daughters, as far as the record goes.

That one son was born a year before Solomon became king, while he was still very young, and Naamah (Rehoboam's mother) was very likely the only wife he really loved, as described so beautifully in his Song of Solomon.

So it is significant that near the end of his life, Solomon is counseling young men to cultivate that special love "with the wife whom thou lovest." The Bible very seldom refers to romantic love or marital love, so this rare reference to romantic love—as between a young bride and bridegroom—is especially noteworthy. The admonition to "live joyfully" is from a word usually translated "alive," so his advice was to keep that young marital love alive and fresh all through life!

Scripture:
Ecclesiastes 9:9; 1 Kings 11:42; Proverbs 5:18-19

God's Mother Heart

*How often would I have gathered thy
children together, even as a hen gathereth
her chickens under her wings.*

The gender most often used in the Bible to describe God is male. However, a few passages refer to His "mother heart" as well. God created both man and woman to bear His image, and both share the divine nature once they're born again.

In the book of Proverbs, wisdom is personified as female and is said to have its source in the Creator. The treasures of wisdom and knowledge are hidden in Christ Jesus, and this helps us understand Christ's statement that He yearned for Jerusalem like a hen for her chicks.

Some have suggested that the virtuous woman of Proverbs 31 shows us what Christ would be like if He had taken human form as a woman. That may or may not be, but the "virtue" of this lady is surely extraordinary. If nothing else, we can acknowledge that this beautiful woman is a magnificent reflection of the mother and wife whose "price is far above rubies."

When we honor our earthly mothers, may we also give thanks to the Creator, who made the unique female nature that reflects the complete and pure love of God for His children.

Scripture:
Matthew 23:37; Genesis 1:27; 2 Peter 1:4;
Colossians 2:3; Proverbs 31

Sweet Naamah

*Behold, thou art fair, my beloved, yea,
pleasant: also our bed is green.*

These words begin King Solomon's tender expressions of
love to his beautiful young wife Naamah. Of the 1005
songs Solomon wrote, he called this one his "song of songs,"
and it clearly centered on his beloved, whom he called "my sister, my spouse," tenderly intimating both their spiritual and
marital relationship.

As Scripture records the annals of the kings, Solomon
and Naamah, whose name means "pleasant," married in their
youth, long before he was married to Pharoah's daughter or
any of his other 700 wives. Naamah was indeed his one true
love.

Solomon called her "fair" and "beloved" and "pleasant."
The Hebrew word for "pleasant" is very similar to "Naamah,"
as though Solomon were calling her by a shortened form of
her name as a term of endearment. The same word is occa-
sionally translated "sweet." Naamah was surely a sweet, pleasant maiden but also a capable woman in mind and heart, fit
to become a queen.

Solomon's song for Naamah is an inspired ode to true
marital love and thus can even be a figurative testimony to the
love of Christ for His church.

Scripture:

Song of Solomon 1:16; 4:9-12; 5:1; 1 Kings 4:32

Evolution and the Woman

*The man is not of the woman: but the woman
of the man. Neither was the man created for
the woman; but the woman for the man.*

In spite of the overwhelming scientific evidence against evolution, some Christians today argue that God used evolution to create. But this position is logically untenable and spiritually dangerous.

One of the most obvious evidences is the unique biblical account of the formation of the body of the first woman. By no stretch of the imagination can this account be harmonized with the so-called evolution of human beings from some earlier group of hominids.

God "formed man of the dust of the ground." Many theistic evolutionists have asserted that this could describe the long, random, and accidental process of evolution. This, of course, is fantasy, not biblical exegesis. There is simply no way for the record of Eve's formation from Adam's side to be so interpreted. Genesis is explicit, and the apostle Paul and Jesus Himself confirm this truth in the New Testament. Both man and woman are special creations of God, not the products of evolutionary development from prehuman animals.

Scripture:
1 Corinthians 11:8-9; Genesis 2:7,21-22;
Matthew 19:4-6; 1 Timothy 2:13

Jephthah's Daughter

*Whatsoever cometh forth of the doors of my
house to meet me…shall surely be the LORD's,
and I will offer it up for a burnt offering.*

Did Jephthah really sacrifice his daughter to God as a burnt offering? The story goes that as Jephthah was preparing to face the Ammonite armies, he made the vow recorded in our text, if God would only give him victory. His beloved daughter was then first to meet him at his return, and so it was she who had to be offered.

However, Hebrews tells us that Jephthah was a man of true faith; he would likely not vow to disobey God's commandments. The problem is that the Hebrew conjunction *waw* (translated "and") varies in meaning depending on context. In this case, "or" is better than "and." Thus, Jephthah vowed that whatever first came out to meet him would be dedicated to the Lord. Hannah made a similar vow and later dedicated her son Samuel.

Thus, Jephthah's daughter, out of love for her father and for God, was dedicated as a perpetual maidservant at the tabernacle. This is an inspiring story of the love that a godly father and daughter had for each other and for their Lord.

Scripture:
Judges 11:31; Hebrews 11:32-33; 1 Samuel 1:11

Made of a Woman

When the fullness of the time was come, God sent forth his Son, made of a woman, made under the law.

This verse in Galatians is key to understanding the incarnation and God's plan of salvation. God promised in Genesis that the seed of the woman would bring salvation from sin and Satan. In God's chosen time, Christ came as Isaiah prophesied, miraculously conceived and born of the virgin.

In Galatians, Paul carefully used the Greek word *ginomai*, translated "made," to indicate the unique nature of Christ's entrance into the world. In fact, His human body had to be specially "prepared" by God so that He could be born with neither an inherent sin nature nor any inherited genetic defects from either parent. Jesus was truly "without blemish and without spot."

He was not only "made of a woman" but also "made under the law" so that He could be shown to live without committing sin. Only through God's written law do we really know what sin is. Therefore, because He was "made under the law" and had come "to fulfill" the law, He can indeed redeem every sinner who will come to Him in repentance and faith.

Scripture:
Galatians 4:4-5; Genesis 3:15; Isaiah 7:14;
Hebrews 10:5; 1 Peter 1:19; Matthew 5:17

David's Great-Grandmother

There is a son born to Naomi; and
they called his name Obed: he is the
father of Jesse, the father of David.

No one knows for certain who wrote the book of Ruth, but it must at least have been written by a contemporary of David. Quite possibly the story was told directly to David himself by his great-grandmother.

When David became king, he must surely have been intrigued by his providential upbringing. He would have been familiar with Jacob's prophecy that someone from the tribe of Judah would rule the children of Israel someday. He must also have marveled at the wonderful grace of God that brought Ruth, a Moabitess, into his ancestry. He undoubtedly noted also that Nahshon, the grandfather of Boaz, was the chief captain of the tribe of Judah when Moses led the Israelites out of Egypt but that he had apparently failed in that role and perished in the wilderness.

David, like Ruth and Nahshon, was brought into the great family of the King. We have too, not because of our own merits, but by His marvelous grace, "not by works of righteousness which we have done, but according to his mercy he saved us."

Scripture:
Ruth 4:17; Genesis 49:8-12; John 1:13;
Titus 3:5; Numbers 1:4-7

The Virtuous Woman

Who can find a virtuous woman? for
her price is far above rubies.

The famous passage in Proverbs 31 on the virtuous woman was originally put together in the form of a Hebrew alphabetic acrostic, as if the writer wanted to pay special tribute to his own mother.

However, "virtuous" has much more meaning than simply moral purity. The Hebrew word, when used as an adjective or adverb describing a woman, was always translated "virtuous" or "virtuously" in the Old Testament. When used in reference to men, however (as it is far more frequently), it is always translated by such words as "strong," "valiant," and "worthy."

Thus, an ideal woman is strong, brave, industrious, and trustworthy. This is woman as God intended woman to be. She is, most especially, a *godly* woman, as our passage states: "Favor is deceitful, and beauty is vain: but a woman that feareth the LORD, she shall be praised."

"Her children arise up, and call her blessed; her husband also, and he praiseth her." This verse is usually acknowledged on Mother's Day, but let us remember that "Honor thy... mother" means every day of the year as well.

Scripture:
Proverbs 31:10-31; Exodus 20:12

The Scarlet Hope

Behold, when we come into the land, thou shalt
bind this line of scarlet thread in the window.

This order was given to Rahab by Joshua's spies, who vowed to protect her and her family. She openly testified, "The LORD your God, he is God in heaven above, and in earth beneath." Hebrews tells us "by faith the harlot Rahab perished not with them that believed not, when she had received the spies with peace."

Rahab was saved because of her faith in God, and she eventually became a member of the family line leading to the Lord Jesus. Her deliverance on the day of Jericho's destruction depended on a "line of scarlet thread" suspended from her window.

This thin, bloodred line constituted a very slender hope for Rahab in the midst of awful judgment, but it was sufficient. Interestingly, the Hebrew word for "line" (found here for the first time in the Bible) is later translated as "hope." Perhaps "line" soon came to mean "hope" because of this very experience, when a "scarlet hope" extended all the way from a repentant sinner to the very God of heaven. David, using the same word, declares in Psalm 71:5, "For thou art my hope, O Lord God."

Scripture:

Joshua 2:11-18; Hebrews 11:31; Matthew 1:5

True Love

And this is love, that we walk
after his commandments.

Love is a perpetually misunderstood concept. The Greeks had three different words for love. Of these, *eros* is not used in the New Testament, yet this is what most people today mean when they speak of love. But love is not made; it is lived.

The word *phileo*, meaning "be fond of," occurs 25 times in the New Testament and about 75 times in various combinations with other words (such as *philadelphia*, or "brotherly love"). *Agape* is the most important and definitive word for love. It is an *active* love, based on intelligent choices.

True love is defined in terms of what it *does*, as we see in 1 Corinthians 13. John wrote in his epistle, "Herein is love, not that we loved God, but that he loved us, and sent his Son to be the propitiation for our sins." True love takes action.

This is seen in true marital love. "Husbands, love your wives, even as Christ also loved the church, and gave himself for it." The Lord Jesus said, "Greater love hath no man than this, that a man lay down his life for his friends." This is true love.

Scripture:

2 John 6; 1 John 4:10; Ephesians 5:25; John 15:13

The Queen of Sheba

*When the queen of Sheba heard of the fame
of Solomon concerning the name of the LORD,
she came to prove him with hard questions.*

A thousand years after the famous visit of Sheba's queen to the court of King Solomon, Jesus declared of her, "The queen of the south shall rise up in the judgment with this generation, and shall condemn it: for she came from the uttermost parts of the earth to hear the wisdom of Solomon; and, behold, a greater than Solomon is here."

The Lord gave Solomon such legendary wisdom that Sheba's queen was compelled to seek out this remarkable leader. He "told her all her questions," so she could testify, "The half was not told me...Blessed be the Lord thy God." He who had given Solomon his great wisdom promises us, "If any of you lack wisdom, let him ask of God, that giveth to all men liberally."

People today turn to every variety of counselors for their training and guidance but refuse to come to the One who is "made unto us wisdom." The "Wonderful Counselor," who is far greater than Solomon, is still inviting all from the uttermost parts of the earth to come.

Scripture:
1 Kings 10:1-9; Matthew 12:42; James 1:5;
1 Corinthians 1:30; Isaiah 9:6

The Clothing of a Virtuous Woman

*Strength and honor are her clothing; and
she shall rejoice in time to come.*

The virtuous woman eulogized in Proverbs 31 is truly an industrious woman who excels in her many endeavors, even in providing clothing for her family. Her own clothing is "silk and purple" because she "layeth her hands to the spindle." She works hard for her family, but more importantly, her spiritual clothing is strength and honor, more lovely even than beautiful garments.

Peter exhorted Christian wives not to emphasize their outward appearance, but rather "the hidden man of the heart, in that which is not corruptible, even the ornament of a meek and quiet spirit, which is in the sight of God of great price."

Likewise the apostle Paul urged "that women adorn themselves in modest apparel" and "with good works."

Thus the exhortation of Scripture is for Christian women to be primarily concerned with their spiritual clothing—strength of character, honor, quietness of spirit, and good works. "Favor is deceitful, and beauty is vain: but a woman that feareth the Lord, she shall be praised."

Scripture:
Proverbs 31; 1 Peter 3:3-4; 1 Timothy 2:9-10

The Wife of Thy Youth

Live joyfully with the wife whom thou
lovest all the days of the life of thy vanity.

We are told that about half of all marriages in our nominally Christian nation end in divorce, despite the fact that most couples at the marriage altar promise to care for each other as long as they both shall live. Some dear friends practiced this for 77 years at the time of his homegoing! They took this promise very seriously.

Of course, many other Bible-believing Christians practice it still, and the Lord Jesus Christ certainly taught it. When a group of Pharisees asked Him if a man could "put away his wife for every cause," the Lord replied, "What therefore God hath joined together, let not man put asunder." In our Scripture text, wise King Solomon counseled every young man to cherish the wife of his youth all the days of his life.

Each February 14, people celebrate Valentine's Day, which has largely been reduced to a day glorifying romantic and sometimes erotic love. Wouldn't it be wonderful if Christians would make their romance a relationship of true Christian love—*agape* love—deep, lasting, and self-sacrificing?

Scripture:
Ecclesiastes 9:9; Matthew 19:6

Hannah's Portion

Unto Hannah he gave a worthy
portion; for he loved Hannah: but
the LORD had shut up her womb.

Elkanah, a Levite, had two wives, Peninnah and Hannah. Peninnah was blessed with sons and daughters by Elkanah, but Hannah was initially barren. This barrenness was not for a lack of love on her husband's part, but rather because "the LORD had shut up her womb."

Hannah took her petition directly to God and "poured out [her] soul before the LORD." Watching this anguished soul was Eli, who was a priest and a judge in Israel. Eli blessed her by asking God to grant her petition. Soon Hannah conceived and delivered a son, whom we know now to be Samuel (which means "asked of God"). Her vow at the time of her petition was to give Samuel back to the Lord.

Consider the outcome of the prayer of this righteous person: The nation of Israel was blessed, God turned the hearts of the people back to Him, and Hannah's desire to be a mother was fulfilled. Her portion from Elkanah was a "worthy portion," but her portion from the Lord was even greater. Expectant prayer to God out of a right heart brings much blessing.

Scripture:
1 Samuel 1:4-15

Love in the Old Testament

*Jacob served seven years for Rachel;
and they seemed unto him but a few
days, for the love he had to her.*

The word "love" in the New Testament almost always refers to unselfish *agape* love. *Eros*, the Greek word for romantic love, is never used in the New Testament. Marital love is ideally *agape* love, as in Paul's exhortation: "Husbands, love your wives, even as Christ also loved the church, and gave himself for it."

The Old Testament uses numerous Hebrew words for "love," and these often have wide variations in meaning, including romantic love. For example, Jacob's willingness to work for Laban seven years in order to obtain Rachel clearly must have involved a high degree of romantic love.

Several different "love" words are used in the Song of Solomon as Solomon and his bride frequently speak of their romantic love for each other. God clearly approves of such love when it is pure and true and involves self-sacrificing *agape* love as well.

The greatest love of all in all the Bible is God's love for the men and women He has created and redeemed.

Scripture:
Genesis 29:20,30; Ephesians 5:25

A Wonderful Mother

Ruth said... Thy people shall be my
people, and thy God my God.

Mothers-in-law don't often receive the honor and respect
that our own mothers do. But they are mothers themselves, and just as wonderful to their own children. The Bible
records the story of Naomi, the honored mother-in-law of
Ruth.

Ruth was living in Moab with Naomi. Naomi and her
husband and their two sons had migrated from Israel to Moab
because of a severe famine in their homeland. But Naomi's
husband and two sons had all died there, leaving Naomi and
two daughters-in-law, Orpah and Ruth. When Naomi felt
she should return to her home in Bethlehem, Ruth insisted
to go with her.

Ruth was willing not only to leave her own country but
even to abandon her pagan Moabite religion and worship
Naomi's God—the true God of Israel—in order to be with
her mother-in-law. What a godly example Naomi must have
been to elicit such love and loyalty from young Ruth!

And the result of Ruth's respect toward Naomi was the
blessing of becoming the bride of Boaz and an ancestor of
King David and thus King Jesus.

Scripture:
Ruth 1:16; 4:21-22

Grandmother Lois

*I call to remembrance the unfeigned faith that is
in thee, which dwelt first in thy grandmother Lois.*

The only grandmother mentioned as such in the Bible was a fine Christian lady named Lois. In fact this is the only time the Greek word *mamme* is used in the Bible. Lois was the maternal grandmother of Paul's young friend Timothy, the man to whom Paul wrote his final and most intimate epistle.

Lois no doubt had influenced her daughter Eunice for Christ, and both had taught and trained young Timothy. Certainly there were many other wonderful grandmothers in the early church, just as there are today.

It is not so well known, however, that Grandparents Day is celebrated in September. God command us, "Honor thy father and mother." They, in turn, have been responsible to honor *their* parents (our grandparents). And one of the greatest blessings God has for godly grandparents is godly grandchildren. "But the mercy of the LORD is...upon them that fear him, and his righteousness unto children's children."

Scripture:
2 Timothy 1:5; 3:14-15; Exodus 20:12;
Ephesians 6:2; Psalm 103:17

Two Mothers

My soul doth magnify the Lord, and my
spirit hath rejoiced in God my Savior.

Two Jewish ladies, each carrying children recently conceived, met to discuss their circumstances. Perhaps billions of mothers before and since have had similar encounters, but this meeting between Mary and Elizabeth was special indeed.

Their conversation turned immediately to God, praising Him for His goodness and grace. No doubt each one experienced all the common difficulties and discomforts of these months, but they chose to dwell on their blessings and the greatness of God.

Mary, especially, burst forth in a torrent of praise, singing of the virtues of her Savior and reveling in His grace. He had chosen her despite her unworthiness, and she focused on communion with her Lord and His gracious dealings with mankind. In all these things, she rejoiced.

These two mothers are examples to all women blessed with childbearing. May each encounter focus on Him, not just on temporal events. May all our fellowship be centered in Him and in His Word, not just with friends or family. May prayer and praise burst forth from our lips, not just idle conversation. May we know all the joy and confidence of Mary and join in her song.

Scripture:
Luke 1:46-55

A Mother's Hands

Every wise woman buildeth her house: but
the foolish plucketh it down with her hands.

Proverbs teaches us what to do and what not to do with our hands. A "little folding of the hands" brings poverty and want (6:10). Hands that "refuse to labor" are slothful hands (21:25). "He becometh poor that dealeth with a slack hand: but the hand of the diligent maketh rich" (10:4). "The hand of the diligent shall bear rule: but the slothful shall be under tribute" (12:24).

The woman of Proverbs 31 "worketh willingly with her hands" (verse 13). "With the fruit of her hands she planteth a vineyard" (verse 16). "She layeth her hands to the spindle" (verse 19). "She stretcheth out her hand to the poor; yea, she reacheth forth her hands to the needy" (verse 20).

The Hebrew word translated "plucketh" in our text means to pull down, or to destroy. It is used in a warlike sense to pull down the wall of a city and destroy it utterly. The plucking down of her house, or its utter destruction, comes when she refuses the children that God has given to build an ongoing testimony. "Lo, children are an heritage of the LORD: and the fruit of the womb is his reward."

Scripture:

Proverbs 14:1; Psalm 127:3

The Mother of Us All

Adam called his wife's name Eve; because
she was the mother of all living.

Sarah, Abraham's wife, was called the mother of "the children of promise," and Noah's wife was the mother of all post-flood mankind, but Eve was "the mother of all living."

Eve experienced the joys and sorrows that all later mothers would know. She evidently had many sons and daughters and probably lived to see many generations of grandchildren. With Adam, she had even known paradise, but sin had entered their lives when they rebelled against God's Word. As a result, God had to say, "In sorrow thou shalt bring forth children."

Nevertheless, as near as we can tell, after her first great sin, Eve trusted God's Word and received His forgiveness and salvation. Later, as the mother of Seth, she taught him about the Lord and all His promises.

Most Christian believers are looking forward to seeing their own mothers again someday and thanking them for bearing them, caring for them, teaching them, and praying for them. But it will be a wonderful experience to meet our first mother also, as well as Sarah, Hannah, Mary, and all the other godly mothers of old.

Scripture:

Genesis 3:16,20; 5:4

Whose Daughters Ye Are

Sarah obeyed Abraham, calling him lord:
whose daughters ye are, as long as ye do well.

Sarah called Abraham "lord," which means "supreme in authority." She was not only obedient but also a woman of faith. "Through faith also Sarah herself received strength to conceive seed, and was delivered of a child when she was past age, because she judged him faithful who had promised."

What makes you a daughter of Sarah? Virtuous behavior, such as suffering patiently. "When ye do well, and suffer for it, ye take it patiently, this is acceptable with God."

In Sarah's most notable example of obedience, she agreed to tell the Philistine king, Abimelech, she was Abraham's sister. In doing so, she "judged him faithful who had promised." She realized the violation of the promised seed of Abraham was at stake, yet she had come to trust the omnipotent God, who expected her to obey and leave the results to Him.

The results? God caused Abimelech to return her untouched to Abraham. "Wherefore let them that suffer according to the will of God commit the keeping of their souls to him in well doing, as unto a faithful Creator."

Scripture:

1 Peter 3:6,17; 2:20; 4:19; Hebrews 11:11; Genesis 20:3,6

Remember Lot's Wife

*His wife looked back from behind
him, and she became a pillar of salt.*

Such a tragic fate for Lot's wife! What events led up to this awful moment? First was Lot's relationship with bad influences. When Abraham offered Lot the choice of where to live, he "pitched his tent toward Sodom" and then moved into the wicked city.

Perhaps the rationale for such compromise was opportunities for the children, more social interaction, or greater security and prosperity. When the angels bring news of Sodom's imminent judgment, Lot is unable to convince his married children to leave. Small wonder that Mrs. Lot looked back to where her dear children and cherished possessions were going up in flames.

Christ spoke of this event: "As it was in the days of Lot; they did eat, they drank, they bought, they sold, they planted, they builded; but the same day that Lot went out of Sodom it rained fire and brimstone from heaven, and destroyed them all." Our focus should not be on the attractions of this world but on that city whose founder and maker is God. The Lord punctuates this prophecy with a poignant instruction: "Remember Lot's wife."

Scripture:
Genesis 19:14-26; 13:10-12; Luke 17:28-32

A Word to the Wives

Wives, be in subjection to your own husbands; that,
if any obey not the word, they also may without
the word be won by the conversation of the wives.

This verse contains a special promise to wives with unsaved husbands. A woman is not to "teach" her husband unless he asks her to do so, so she must first witness to him "without a word," letting her "chaste conversation" (that is, manner of living) "coupled with fear" (that is, due honor and respect for her husband) do her witnessing for her. The "ornament of a meek and quiet spirit, which is in the sight of God of great price" can become a beautiful "adorning," which will eventually convince a stubborn mind and win a hardened heart.

Note also the emphasis on "your own husbands." A Christian wife in this circumstance may unconsciously compare her husband to her pastor or other Christian male acquaintances. But this is not the will of God and is not the way to win her husband to Christ.

This is a conditional promise. It may take time, for the wife's behavior must be tested with time, but the divine promise is that husbands will "without the word be won by the conversation of the wives."

Scripture:

1 Peter 3:1-4; 1 Timothy 2:12; 1 Corinthians 14:34-35

The Clothing of a Godly Woman

Strength and honor are her clothing; and
she shall rejoice in time to come.

A lovely little song of the 1930s was called "Try a Little Tenderness." You may not be familiar with it, but if you have had a caring, self-sacrificing mother, you can relate to one of its stanzas: "She may be weary: women do get weary, wearing that same shabby dress. And when she's weary, try a little tenderness."

I had such a mother, and this familiar chapter on the virtuous woman always reminds me of her. As essentially the main support of three young sons in a depression-era divorced household, she managed to provide food, clothing, and shelter for the family by a succession of low-paying jobs and with little thought of her own needs.

Many women today, on the other hand, seem concerned mainly with their own personal appearance and on being well dressed, spending freely on the latest fashions. But a godly woman is one whose apparel is "strength and honor."

Peter said their apparel should "not be that outward adorning of plaiting the hair, and of wearing of gold, or of putting on of apparel," but rather "the ornament of a meek and quiet spirit, which is in the sight of God of great price."

Scripture:
Proverbs 31:10-31; 1 Peter 3:3-4

Who Is the Strange Woman?

The lips of a strange woman drop as an honeycomb,
and her mouth is smoother than oil: but her end is
bitter as wormwood, sharp as a two-edged sword.

The "strange woman" is actually any woman not instructed in the laws of God, as were the women of Israel, and consequently who practices and encourages idolatrous promiscuity.

This "strange woman" is the subject of at least six urgent warnings in Proverbs. Solomon allowed his marriages with such foreign women to finally lead him and his nation into deadly compromise. "King Solomon loved many strange women…his wives turned away his heart after other gods… And Solomon did evil in the sight of the LORD."

These warnings in Proverbs apply today to any believer who might be tempted to become involved romantically or sexually with an unbeliever.

In contrast, the virtuous woman is personified as wisdom, and the great theme of Proverbs is the vital importance of true wisdom. In the ultimate sense, of course, folly is none other than the lure of Satan, for "her house is the way to hell, going down to the chambers of death." But wisdom becomes Christ, for wisdom personified says, "Whoso findeth me findeth life."

Scripture:
Proverbs 5:3; 1:20-33; 7:27; 8:35; 1 Kings 11:1-8

The Steadfast Faith of
Joseph and Mary

There was no room for them in the inn.

Most of us have never been stranded without shelter for a short time—let alone have had to give birth in an animal pen. We will never have to know just how isolated and abandoned Joseph and Mary must have felt that first Christmas Eve.

Both of them had received personal visits from the chief angel, Gabriel, and knew that the Father of this Child was none other than the Holy Spirit. And both of them had obeyed God's instruction. They had every reason to expect special treatment and recognition for their faith and obedience.

Instead, however, the false rumors about Mary's infidelity continued to swirl around them, and the long trek from Nazareth to Bethlehem only added to their plight. The Bible does not tell us how long they looked for shelter—we are only told that "while they were there," Mary had to deliver the Child and lay Him in a manger.

And until the shepherds came with their wonderful story of the angelic chorus, Joseph and Mary had no word of verification. Yet their steadfast faith allowed them to see God's plan unfold through their lives.

Scripture:
Luke 1:38; 2:6-7; Matthew 1:18-24

Jesus in Mary's Womb

The LORD…formed me from the
womb to be His servant.

Seven hundred years before Jesus' incarnation, he was prophetically referred to as One who would be formed in a womb. Of course, as divine Son, He existed from all eternity, but it was not until an appointed time in history that He started as fully human—in His mother's womb. The angel said to Mary, "The Holy Ghost shall come upon thee, and the power of the Highest shall overshadow thee: therefore also that holy thing which shall be born of thee shall be called the Son of God."

Of course, human prenatal life has today been given a secular description. Evolutionists try to explain that human life before birth is tracing out its evolutionary history, but this is a sad delusion. Jesus was never a fish or a frog, and neither were any of us.

He, the Creator, became a baby and lived for a while in a virgin's womb so that as a man He could go to a cross and reverse Adam's fall. By His perfect obedience to the Father, He also offers human beings eternal life. May we celebrate life now and forever!

Scripture:

Isaiah 49:5; John 1:1; Galatians 4:4; Luke 1:35

Mary on Easter Morning

*The first day of the week cometh Mary Magdalene
early, when it was yet dark, unto the sepulchre,
and seeth the stone taken away from the sepulchre.*

Most of the events regarding our Lord's ministry on earth are not found in all of the Gospels, but all reveal that Mary Magdalene was at the tomb early on the first Easter morning.

She is first mentioned as one out of whom were cast seven devils. Along with several other women, she attached herself to Christ's entourage as He traveled about, and they "ministered unto him of their substance."

His disciples forsook and denied Him, but she was present at His crucifixion. She was still with Him as He was removed from the cross and laid in the tomb. She organized the effort to anoint the body with spices after the Sabbath. And what was her reward? "Now when Jesus was risen early the first day of the week, he appeared first to Mary Magdalene."

Mary may have experienced these events firsthand, but because of what Christ did, we can likewise experience His resurrected presence and Spirit, participate in the same joyous ministry, and welcome Him when He returns.

Scripture:
John 20:1,18; Mark 16:9; Matthew 27:55-61;
Luke 8:1-3; 23:56; Acts 1:12-14

Mary's Savior

Mary said, My soul doth magnify the Lord, and
my spirit hath rejoiced in God my Savior.

Jesus' mother rejoiced because of Jesus, but like any mother, she grieved when she saw her special Son humiliated by the crowd and the soldiers and then nailed to a cross. Jesus could have come down and stood beside her. He had power to do so, she knew. Why didn't He?

Instead, He chose to meet a far greater need. Mary wanted her Son, but she needed her Savior. She needed more than emotional peace on earth. She needed eternal peace. And even as Jesus commanded John to care for His mother after He was gone, He was doing something for Mary vastly more profound.

He remained on the cross to save His mother from her sins. He wanted her and every other sinner to be with Him in heaven forever, and He was and is the only Savior possible. Mary herself confessed a need for a Savior: "My spirit hath rejoiced in God my Savior."

By grace through faith, each of us enters heaven only because Mary's Son suffered death on a cross. Mary's tears have indeed turned to joy. She's now in heaven with her Son and Savior, the Lord Jesus Christ.

Scripture:
Luke 1:46-47; John 19:25-27; 17:24

Mary's Alabaster Box

Then took Mary a pound of ointment of spikenard,
very costly, and anointed the feet of Jesus.

This scene reveals a lot about the depth of Mary's spiritual understanding. Mary was interested in spiritual things, and as she "sat at Jesus' feet and, heard his word," He said that "Mary hath chosen that good part, which shall not be taken away from her."

Her conduct after the death of Lazarus revealed her faith, for Martha ran to meet the Lord, "but Mary sat still in the house." However, when she received the summons from Jesus, "she arose quickly, and came to him." Her words expressed her heartfelt belief: "If thou hadst been here, my brother had not died."

By the time of this anointing, Mary's spiritual understanding and faith had matured. Did she sense that her burial ointment would be of no use if not used that day? Who can say? But the fact remains that the only anointing Jesus received was prior to His death. Would that our spiritual eyes were as open as Mary's and our actions guided by faith such as hers.

Scripture:

John 11:20-45; 12:3,7; Luke 10:39-42; Matthew 20:2

Martha's Motives

Lord, dost thou not care that my sister
hath left me to serve alone?

Jesus "loved Martha" and cared so much that He used this opportunity to teach her the key to Christian service. "Martha, Martha, thou art careful and troubled about many things." Jesus did not address what Martha was *doing*, but what she was *thinking* while she worked.

Martha was anxious to the point of distraction. This was Martha's state of mind as she served. On the other hand, Jesus said, "Mary hath chosen that good part, which shall not be taken away from her." What was Mary doing? She "sat at Jesus' feet, and heard his word."

Many things can be taken away from us, but if we have heard God's Word and have made it part of our lives, that word can never be taken away. "The word of the Lord endureth for ever." When God's Word is the basis of our thoughts and our service, we shall never "suffer loss" in the fire that shall try men's work. Martha wasn't wrong because of *what* she was doing, but because of *why* she did it. Mary served her Master far better by showing us we need to first sit at "Jesus' feet," the source of service.

Scripture:
Luke 10:38-42; John 11:5; 1 Peter 1:25

Elkanah and Hannah

*Elkanah her husband said unto her, Do what
seemeth thee good; tarry until thou have weaned
him; only the LORD establish his word.*

The final clause of this verse might seem misplaced. Elkanah surely desired the establishment of God's word through His servant Eli prior to Samuel's birth, but what could he have meant after God's promise had been fulfilled?

Hannah's request for a son seemed to transcend time. If the Lord would give her a son, she promised to return him to the Lord's service. And so Samuel, the son given, was eventually the one to anoint David as King over Israel.

Hannah's prayer in the following chapter is saturated with faith and hope. Her heart was bursting with love and adoration for God's majesty and goodness: "There is none holy as the LORD: for there is none beside thee." Elkanah was also bonded to the Lord in faith. He led his family in worship and told Hannah, "Only the LORD establish his word."

How profoundly was the word established! The Lord took on human flesh—Jehovah God Incarnate! Elkanah's hope was fulfilled, and Hannah's Mighty King and Messiah reigns now.

Scripture:
1 Samuel 1:3,21,23; 2:2

Priscilla and Aquila

*Aquila and Priscilla…expounded unto
him the way of God more perfectly.*

What does a loving Christian marriage really look like? Aquila and Priscilla give us insight into what married love is all about and what it can do.

These two first met Paul in Corinth following the expulsion of all Jews from Rome in AD 49, and they evidently became two of his dearest friends. In business as tentmakers like Paul, they invited him to live with them, allowing him freedom to teach.

Although the exact time is debated, it is likely that sometime during the stay in Corinth they risked their lives for Paul, for he later wrote, "Greet Priscilla and Aquila my helpers in Christ Jesus: who have for my life laid down their own necks: unto whom not only I give thanks, but also all the churches of the Gentiles."

We don't know all the details, but we do know that they served God effectually together for years. And perhaps this is what a truly loving Christian marriage is all about: serving, teaching, hosting, evangelizing, discipling, working, sacrificing, praying, suffering, traveling—together, always together—for a lifetime. That's a marriage that honors God!

Scripture:
Acts 18:2-4,26; Romans 16:3-4

Weep Not, O Rachel!

*Refrain thy voice from weeping, and thine eyes
from tears: for thy work shall be rewarded.*

Afraid for his throne, King Herod "slew all the children
that were in Bethlehem, and in all the coasts thereof,
from two years old and under." These children died for Jesus,
who later would die for them. As a result, "in Ramah was there
a voice heard, lamentation, and weeping, and great mourning,
Rachel weeping for her children, and would not be comforted,
because they are not."

Rachel, Jacob's beloved wife, had died in Bethlehem, and
the grieving mothers of Bethlehem's slaughtered children were
all personified in her name. Significantly, this event had been
prophesied long before: "Then was fulfilled that which was
spoken by Jeremiah the prophet."

Jeremiah's prophecy includes the words of comfort in our
text above: "Refrain thy voice from weeping." The slain children were too young for conscious sin, and Christ's blood cov-
ers their innate sin, so they are safe with the Lord. Surely all
small children who die (before or after birth) are secure in
Christ, awaiting His second coming and their own resurrection!

Scripture:
Jeremiah 31:15-16; Matthew 2:16-18; Genesis 35:19

If I Perish

So will I go in unto the king, which is not according to the law: and if I perish, I perish.

This is the courageous testimony of Queen Esther as she prepared to risk her own life in order to save the lives of her people. It was a capital crime for anyone to intrude into the king's throne room unbidden, but she was willing to do so in order to do the will of God, knowing that "we ought to obey God rather than men."

Shadrach, Meshach, and Abednego were willing to enter the fiery furnace rather than worship the gods of Babylon, declaring, "Our God whom we serve is able to deliver us from the burning fiery furnace, and he will deliver us out of thine hand, O king. But if not, be it known unto thee, O king, that we will not serve thy gods."

God did deliver Esther and the three Jewish youths, but many through the ages have chosen to die rather than deny their faith. All the apostles except John died as martyrs, for example, and so have countless others throughout the centuries.

If a similar choice should ever confront us, may God give us the grace to say with Esther, "If I perish, I perish."

Scripture:
Esther 4:16; Acts 5:29; Daniel 3:17-18

The Virgin Birth

All this was done, that it might be fulfilled
which was spoken of the Lord by the prophet,
saying, Behold, a virgin shall be with child.

The apostle Matthew is in this passage citing God's great prophecy in Isaiah: "Behold, a virgin shall conceive, and bear a son, and shall call his name Immanuel." In this verse, the Hebrew word for "virgin" is *almah*. A number of Bible versions have translated this simply as "young woman," and many theological liberals use this translation as a way to deny the virgin birth of Christ.

Some commentators have tried to find modern parallels in processes such as artificial insemination, parthenogenesis, and others, but no other true virgin birth has been recorded in all human history. It is a human impossibility but a divine miracle.

In our text above, Matthew translated *almah* by the Greek word *parthenos*, which can only mean "virgin." Mary and Joseph, of course, understood it that way. And so did Paul when he wrote to the Galatians.

The conception and birth of Jesus did indeed require a mighty miracle. But how else could the infinite God ever become a man?

Scripture:
Matthew 1:20-23; Isaiah 7:14; Galatians 4:4

She Shall Be Praised

Favor is deceitful, and beauty is vain: but a
woman that feareth the LORD, she shall be praised.

Proverbs 31 is identified as "the words of King Lemuel." It is divided into two distinct parts, so some have proposed that it has two different authors. The first part (verses 1-9) consists of "the prophecy that his mother taught him," and the second part (verses 10-31) describes "a virtuous woman."

"Many daughters have done virtuously." Ruth was described as a virtuous woman, and this gives us insight into such a woman's character. The woman described in Proverbs 31 has achieved the glory of her womanhood in all its fullness, both in the home as wife and mother, and in her community. Not only do her children bless her, but her husband has absolute confidence in her and appreciates the bounty she brings. He has the freedom to be an effective leader in the community and praises her virtue to others.

What was her secret? She fears the Lord, and her reverence of God allows her inner beauty and diligence to blossom so that, by wisdom and devotion, she is honored and praised and blessed by her husband and her children.

Scripture:

Proverbs 31; Ruth 3:11

Children Call Her Blessed

Her children arise up, and call her blessed;
her husband also, and he praiseth her.

The last 22 verses of Proverbs 31 comprise an acrostic poem, with each verse beginning with the corresponding letter of the 22-letter Hebrew alphabet. The theme is the virtuous woman, so this passage has been the subject of countless Mother's Day sermons about the ideal wife and mother.

The Old Testament judge Deborah was also surely a valiant, strong, and godly woman as well as a great "mother in Israel."

In his proverbs, Solomon had written sober warnings against the "strange woman" (2:16), the "foolish woman" (9:13), the "brawling woman" (21:9), the "contentious woman" (21:19), the "odious woman" (30:23), the "whorish woman" (6:26), and the "evil woman" (6:24), possibly thinking of his unhappy marriages to his 700 pagan wives, starting with "the daughter of Pharaoh."

But it is fitting and touching that he closed his book of Proverbs with the beautiful soliloquy on the strong, pure, energetic, wise, valiant, and virtuous woman, who has come to be the ideal wife and mother role model for godly women in every age.

Scripture:
Proverbs 31; Judges 5:7; 1 Kings 11:1-3

Unbreakable Love

*Therefore shall a man leave his father
and his mother, and shall cleave unto
his wife: and they shall be one flesh.*

When the Pharisees asked Jesus for His view on divorce, He replied by quoting our text, giving the Creator's view on marriage. He added, "What therefore God hath joined together, let not man put asunder."

In some special way, known fully only to Him, a man and woman in a marriage relationship can truly become one flesh, just as Adam and Eve were one flesh after Eve had been fashioned from Adam's side.

And just as we are inseparably "members of his body, of his flesh, and of his bones," as Paul reminds us, God designed each of us to be inseparably "one flesh" with his or her spouse.

Paul uses a forceful word for "leave," meaning to completely leave one's parents and "be joined" to the spouse. This word is equally forceful and leaves no room for a halfhearted commitment.

Marriage partners, in the eyes of the Creator, should be inseparable, just as the bones and flesh of a body cannot be separated, and just as we cannot be separated from Him.

Scripture:
Genesis 2:23-24; Matthew 19:4-6;
Ephesians 5:30-31; Romans 8:35-39

Kisses and Tears

*The LORD grant you that ye may find
rest... Then she kissed them; and they
lifted up their voice, and wept.*

When Naomi decided to return to Israel from Moab after the death of her husband and her two married sons, one of her daughters-in-law decided to return to her own household, prompting both kissing and weeping.

Kissing was common in those days when departing. Laban complained when Jacob and his family left secretly and had "not suffered me to kiss my sons and my daughters." Later on, however, he "kissed his sons and his daughters, and blessed them."

The Christians in Ephesus "all wept sore, and fell on Paul's neck, and kissed him" at his departure. The same word for fervent kissing is used of the woman with the alabaster box of ointment who washed Jesus' feet with her tears, kissing his feet. And the father of the prodigal son kissed him upon his return home. And of course, Judas betrayed the Lord with a kiss.

These expressions of emotion, love, and concern are still appropriate today, especially when the kiss is a "holy kiss" and the tears are tears of love.

Scripture:

Ruth 1:1-9; Genesis 31:27-28,55; Acts 20:36-37;
Luke 7:38; 15:20; Mark 14:45; Romans 16:16

The Man Child

She brought forth a man child, who was
to rule all nations with a rod of iron.

In his heavenly vision from the Lord, the apostle John saw an amazing sight in heaven—a woman "clothed with the sun...travailing in birth" with "a great red dragon" awaiting "to devour her child as soon as it was born."

The figure of the man child clearly refers to Jesus Christ because He alone will "rule all nations with a rod of iron." The vision, in fact, dramatizes the long warfare between the great dragon, Satan, and the seed of the woman, prophesied in Genesis.

When Christ returns from heaven, all believers, living and dead, will be "caught up" to meet Him in the air, and thus may well be included in the man child of the great sign.

There has been continuous warfare between the seed of the serpent and the spiritual seed of the woman. The dragon is forever "wroth with the woman" and with "the remnant of her seed, which keep the commandments of God, and have the testimony of Jesus Christ." But Christ will finally prevail and cast Satan into the eternal lake of fire.

Scripture:
Revelation 12:1-9,17; 19:15; 20:10; Genesis 3:15;
1 Thessalonians 4:17

From a Child

From a child thou hast known the holy scriptures.

A child who is being taught the Bible, such as little Timothy was, has a wonderful advantage. Statistics have shown that most genuinely Christian adults accepted Christ while still young. And, as in Timothy's case, mothers usually carry most of the responsibility for teaching the Scriptures to their children.

Paul and Timothy met when Timothy was a young man, and he must have made quite an impression. Years later, Paul told Timothy, "I call to remembrance the unfeigned faith that is in thee, which dwelt first in thy grandmother Lois, and thy mother Eunice."

Other godly adults may well exert a great influence for good in a child's life, but a mother who loves the Lord, studies the Scriptures, and teaches them to her children has a value "far above rubies" and receives a double reward—first when she sees her children grow spiritually strong and fruitful, then later when she will surely hear her own loving Savior say, "Well done, thou good and faithful servant."

May today's young mothers seek diligently to follow in the spiritual footsteps of Eunice and Lois!

Scripture:
2 Timothy 3:15; 1:5; Proverbs 31:10; Matthew 25:21,23

Carest Thou Not?

They awake him, and say unto him,
Master, carest thou not that we perish?

Have you ever wondered in times of great adversity if Jesus really cares? There is no need to doubt. God cares about the sparrow, and He surely cares about His own dear children.

When the disciples thought Jesus didn't care, He said, "Why are ye so fearful? How is it that ye have no faith?" When Mary and Martha complained about Jesus' delay to help Lazarus, He told them, "If thou wouldest believe, thou shouldest see the glory of God."

A woman of Canaan cried out to Him for mercy for her demon-possessed daughter, "but he answered her not a word." He seemed not to care, but she kept calling on Him until He finally said, "O woman, great is thy faith: be it unto thee even as thou wilt."

The twelve disciples, Mary and Martha, and the Canaanite woman all wondered if Jesus really cared. But in the end, He calmed the storm, raised Lazarus, and healed the girl, and their faith was strengthened.

Peter wrote, "The trial of your faith…though it be tried with fire, might be found unto praise and honor and glory at the appearing of Jesus Christ." Amen.

Scripture:
Mark 4:38-40; John 11:40; Matthew 15:23,28; 1 Peter 1:7

The Deception of Eve

Adam was not deceived, but the woman
being deceived was in the transgression.

Yea, hath God said?" These words are the first glimpse of
Satan in the Bible, although Scripture teaches that he
already had been at his work of deception in the heavenly
realm, where a third of the angelic host followed him in rebellion against God. His own pride deceived him into believing
he could be "like the most High," and he used the same tactic
on Eve, telling her, "ye shall be as gods."

Eve was created by God's own hand and was perfect. She
and Adam enjoyed a perfect world, free from sin. When she
disobeyed God, she threw away everything good—her home,
her provisions, her fellowship with the Creator, her perfect
love for Adam, and eventually her own life.

Eve may have been the first to be deceived into throw-
ing away all she could hope for, but she was certainly not the
last. Whether for physical gratification, esthetic pleasure, or
intellectual pride, millions still reject the Creator and are, like
Eve, "without excuse." But ultimately Eve knew that one day
the promised seed would conquer sin and death for her and
for all the world.

Scripture:
1 Timothy 2:14; Isaiah 14:12-14;
Genesis 3:1-5; 4:25; Romans 1:20

Particular Mercy

*Somebody hath touched me: for I perceive
that virtue is gone out of me.*

With crowds pressing in, the Lord Jesus was on His way to restore a young girl. But the need of another temporarily intervened. A woman reached out "and touched the border of his garment" and was healed immediately.

"Somebody hath touched me," He said. The disciples told Him that everybody was pressing in on Him, but the Lord perceived that "virtue" (power) had left Him. Jesus turned and told the woman, "Daughter, be of good comfort: thy faith hath made thee whole; go in peace." And then Jesus turned his attention back to the little girl in need, and she too was restored.

We must remember that when our Lord was on the cross, He was not simply dying for humanity. Rather, He died particularly for Peter, James, John, and every other human being, including you and me.

Jesus no doubt perceived virtue going out from Him for all His sheep individually down through the ages. What a wonderful Savior we have! He knows our names. He died for us individually on the cross and intercedes individually for us now.

Scripture:
Luke 8:43-54; Hebrews 7:25

Bitter Grace

Call me not Naomi, call me Mara: for the
Almighty hath dealt very bitterly with me.

Naomi lost her husband and two grown sons while sojourning in Moab. She had little hope left but soon saw the sweetness of the Lord in her life after returning to her home in Israel, especially through Ruth and through her descendants.

Blessings had actually begun for Naomi before she spoke these words. Ruth, her daughter-in-law, had already professed allegiance toward Naomi's God and had chosen to make her home with Naomi and to serve her the rest of her days.

The beautiful romance that developed between Ruth and Boaz—a man of great faith—eventually led to their marriage and to a son, Obed. Obed was the grandfather of King David, and David's prophesied "Son" is Jesus, the promised Messiah. The bitterness of Naomi became sweet grace that blessed the entire world. The Scriptures say that one day every tear will be wiped away and death itself will be abolished. Bitterness will become blessing.

The sweetest truth of all, however, is to be united by faith to the One who long ago took our bitterness to give us His sweetness.

Scripture:
Ruth 1:20; 4:22; Matthew 1:1; Revelation 21:4

How to Train a Child

Train up a child in the way he should go: and
when he is old, he will not depart from it.

The Hebrew word translated "train up" (*chanak*) is elsewhere always rendered "dedicate." Our children are to be
"dedicated" to a certain calling and then trained specifically for
that purpose.

But what is this calling? Parents often mistakenly try to
lead their children into ways of *their* own choosing. Dad wants
his son to follow his profession, Mom wants her daughter to
marry a wealthy man, and every child will have his or her
own ambitions. "The way he should go," however, is the way
the Lord wants a child to follow. Hannah dedicated her child
Samuel to the service of the Lord, and he was specially trained
by Eli the priest. We too should recognize that the Lord has
designed a specific purpose for each of our kids.

It is vital that parents dedicate their children to the Lord's
way from an early age, discerning God's leading, recognizing
the distinctiveness of their children, and encouraging them
in the way of the Lord. God's promise is that at the end of
their lives, our children will have had a productive career He
has chosen.

Scripture:

Proverbs 22:6

The Return to the Upper Room

When they were come in, they went up into
an upper room... These all continued with
one accord in prayer and supplication.

Myriad thoughts must have swirled about the believers as they returned to the upper room after Christ's ascension. Despite their enemies in Jerusalem, they knew Jesus' authority—"all power is given unto me in heaven and in earth"—and His protection would be with them "even unto the end of the world."

Those present included the 11 remaining disciples. Peter, who had denied the Lord, was abundantly forgiven. Thomas' doubts were answered. And John, "the disciple whom Jesus loved," returned after deserting Jesus in the garden. Mary, of course, was there. How glorious to see Him resurrected and ascended after the crushing anguish of watching Him die! The entire gathering was a trophy of His grace, mercy, and forgiveness.

Notice they joined together in "one accord," a common bond of faith and purpose, praying and petitioning God for direction, peace, and power. What a lesson for each of us to remain steadfast and hopeful for God to work His will in our lives!

Scripture:
Acts 1:13-14; Matthew 28:18-20

Praise at the Incarnation

*Blessed be the Lord God of Israel; for he
hath visited and redeemed his people, and
hath raised up an horn of salvation for
us in the house of his servant David.*

These words of praise by Zacharias at the birth of John the
Baptist comprise one of seven doxologies given in light of
Jesus' entrance into the human family. Mary, the mother of
Jesus, proclaimed, "My soul doth magnify the Lord, and my
spirit hath rejoiced in God my Savior." But the first doxol-
ogy was spoken by John's mother, Elizabeth: "Blessed art thou
among women, and blessed is the fruit of thy womb."

The shepherds, who saw the newborn Jesus, "returned,
glorifying and praising God." Eight days later, at Jesus' circumcision in Jerusalem, the aged Simeon "blessed God, and
said…mine eyes have seen thy salvation, which thou hast prepared before the face of all people." The prophetess Anna "gave
thanks likewise unto the Lord, and spake of him to all them
that looked for redemption in Jerusalem."

Finally, about two years later, the wise men from the east
"fell down, and worshipped him." Humble Jewish shepherds
and great Gentile scholars joined with priest and prophet and
godly women to utter praise for the gift of His Son. Can we
do any less?

Scripture:
Luke 1:42-69; 2:20-38; Matthew 2:11

The Immediacy of the Lord's Work

*He stood over her, and rebuked the
fever; and it left her: and immediately
she arose and ministered unto them.*

Luke describes the healing of Peter's mother-in-law as only a physician could. Her fever had been severe, he describes, but her healing by Jesus was remarkable. Peter's wife probably witnessed her mother's healing. Notice the immediacy of the Lord's work. Normally, when people recover from a fever, they need time to fully recuperate. But here we read that "immediately she arose and ministered unto them." Only the Lord can administer healing such as this.

The healing mercy of the Lord Jesus was always instantly effective. Dr. Luke records Him healing both a leper and a paralytic immediately. Later, we read that a woman who had suffered from a continual flow of blood for 12 years was healed immediately, and a little girl who was dead "arose straightway."

And when Jesus stood and spoke before His friend's dead body in the tomb, Lazarus came forth. How effective is the healing of the Great Physician!

Scripture:

Luke 4:39; 5:13,25; 8:44,55; John 11:43

59

A Canaanite Dog

*It is not meet to take the children's
bread, and to cast it to dogs.*

What kind of words are these to say to a woman seeking God's mercy? The Lord Jesus had just referred to Jews as lost sheep, but then He referred to this woman, and Gentiles in general, as dogs.

Undoubtedly Jesus was testing the woman, and probably the disciples as well. She had come to plead for her daughter's life but perhaps did not realize the utter poverty of her own condition. But rather than take offense, she bowed before Jesus with great faith. The Scripture says, "God resisteth the proud, but giveth grace unto the humble." And He surely did reward her, for from that moment, "her daughter was made whole."

We do well to humble ourselves before the words of the master and not to take offense. Our responsibility is to wait upon Him—to bow our hearts before Him and persevere in prayer. And His example is ours, to "follow his steps" with humility and trust in the One who judges righteously.

Scripture:

Matthew 15:24-28; James 4:6; Isaiah 40:31; Luke 18:1;
1 Peter 2:21-25

An Anointing Memorial

There came unto him a woman having
an alabaster box of very precious
ointment, and poured it on his head.

Even small acts of love and concern can have eternal impact. Mary of Bethany, Martha's sister, was prompted to give Jesus a very precious box filled with spikenard ointment. She broke open the box and poured the oil over Jesus' head while He sat eating at the home of Simon the leper.

Sadly, the disciples, and especially Judas, failed to grasp the significance of the gesture, complaining that it wasted resources. But Jesus rebuked them, explaining that Mary's act was "a good work" that would be remembered throughout the whole world. Her expression of love for Jesus was a timely act of sacrifice, for He knew He would soon be departed from them.

What can be said for sacrificial giving to the cause of Christ? First, that He should be the focus of our attention in all that we do; second, that we should give our best to Him in gifts and service; and lastly, that our love for Jesus can result in good works that have eternal impact, for He looks at the heart.

Scripture:
Matthew 26:7-13; Luke 10:39; John 12:3,5

The Alabaster Box

*There came a woman having an alabaster
box of ointment…and she brake the
box, and poured it on his head.*

John reveals that this woman was Mary of Bethany, sister of
Lazarus and Martha, who "anointed the feet of Jesus, and
wiped his feet with her hair: and the house was filled with the
odor of the ointment."

Today, that lovely container and its aromatic contents
would be worth hundreds of dollars. Yet Mary gladly broke
her alabaster box—so it could never be used again—and
poured its costly perfume over her Lord, from His head to His
feet, thus anointing His whole body. Then, as the ointment
ran down to His feet, she wiped them clean with her long hair.

Little did the disciples know that in just one week His
battered body would be laid in a grave, anointed with myrrh
instead of spikenard, and wrapped in burial linens instead of
Mary's hair. But Jesus knew, and Mary had "done what she
could" to show the reality of her love for her Lord. It had cost
her dearly, not only in material possessions but also in sacrifice of all pride and self-esteem, and the Lord was honored.

Scripture:
Mark 14:3-8; John 12:3; Matthew 26:10-13

God My Personal Savior

My spirit hath rejoiced in God my Savior.

One of the most wonderful titles of the Lord Jesus Christ is that of Savior. The Greek word *soter* occurs 24 times in the New Testament and is applied only to Christ, "for there is none other name under heaven given among men, whereby we must be saved."

It is significant that this first use of *soter* in our text above recognizes that our Savior can be none other than God Himself—"God my Savior"—and also that this fact should cause our spirits to rejoice, as Mary's did. He is also "the Savior of the world"—His work on the cross is sufficient to save all who will receive Him.

There are many today who see the man Jesus as a great teacher and example but reject His deity. There are many others who believe in a cosmic deity of some kind but are unwilling to believe that He could become uniquely incarnate in a perfect man. How urgent it is that we believe that our Creator must also become our Savior. Then with Mary, each of us can say, "My spirit hath rejoiced in God my Savior."

Scripture:

Luke 1:47; Acts 4:12; John 4:42; 1 John 4:14

Adorned with Good Works

...not with broided hair, or gold, or pearls,
or costly array; but...with good works.

Christians are under great pressure to compromise with worldly standards. The apostle Paul is addressing public worship in our passage, but these principles have broader application and are much needed today. Women are to wear "modest apparel," appropriate to the occasion. Few Christian women understand the struggles men undergo with their thoughts, triggered by their eyes. A worship service should be a refuge for all who are there to focus on the Lord.

Likewise, women's outer appearance should be reverent or respectful, not attracting attention to themselves, but focusing attention on God. "Sobriety" implies self-control and sound judgment, reflecting the true inner character of the woman.

The adornment "which becometh women professing godliness" is "good works." These works certainly are not limited to duties within the worship service, but are outward manifestations of an inner Christian character and may be known specifically only to God. All Christians, Scripture tells us, should live in such a way "that they may adorn the doctrine of God our Savior in all things."

Scripture:
1 Timothy 2:8-10; Titus 2:10

The Fourfold Restoring

*He shall restore the lamb fourfold, because he
did this thing, and because he had no pity.*

King David desired a married woman, Bathsheba, even
though her husband, Uriah, was one of his own "mighty
men." When their adultery resulted in her pregnancy, David
schemed to have Uriah killed on the battlefield. "But the thing
that David had done displeased the LORD."

To bring him to acknowledge his sin, the prophet Nathan
told him of a rich man who had stolen the only lamb of a poor
servant to feed his guests even though he himself had an abundance of flocks. Indignantly, David pronounced the judgment
found in our text, demanding a fourfold restoration from the
rich man. "Thou art the man," said Nathan, and David did
repent in great shame, acknowledging his sin.

God forgave him because of this, but David eventually experienced the fourfold judgment he himself had pronounced. First, Bathsheba's child died. Then came the rape of
his virgin daughter, Tamar, by her half brother Amnon. This
led to Amnon's murder by her brother Absalom. And finally
this resulted in the rebellion and death of Absalom. We need
to remember God's ancient warning: "Be sure your sin will
find you out."

Scripture:

2 Samuel 12:6-18; 23:8,39; 11:27; 13:1,14,28-29; 18:9,14;
Numbers 32:23

That Holy Thing

The angel answered and said unto her…
that holy thing which shall be born of
thee shall be called the Son of God.

What a miracle was the conception of the incarnate God in Mary's womb! Notice that the angel Gabriel calls the developing baby "that holy thing." The birth of Jesus, of course, had to be a perfectly normal human birth, carried full term from conception to birth, for "in all things it behooved him to be made like unto his brethren."

Jesus' growing body in Mary's womb was—apart from innate sin—truly human from the moment of conception, and this can be said of every human embryo.

The idea that the fetus becomes human only after the first trimester or even later is based on the infamous recapitulation theory of the nineteenth-century evolutionists, who taught that the embryo recapitulated the evolutionary history of an animal ancestry. This bizarre and long-discredited notion is still offered as alleged proof of evolution and as the pseudo-scientific rationale for abortion. No knowledgeable embryologist teaches such a thing today, of course.

Abortion is contrary to Scripture and the purposes of God, and it is wholly unscientific as well.

Scripture:
Luke 1:35; Hebrews 2:17

Altogether Lovely

*His mouth is most sweet: yea, he is altogether
lovely. This is my beloved, and this is my
friend, O daughters of Jerusalem.*

Solomon's beautiful marital song is, at least in part, an allegory depicting the love between Christ and His bride, the
church, "which he hath purchased with his own blood."

Only of Christ can it truly be said that "he is altogether
lovely." Even those who rejected His love "wondered at the
gracious words which proceeded out of his mouth." The
psalmist prophetically sang, "Thou art fairer than the children of men: grace is poured into thy lips."

As the bride gives her testimony concerning her beloved,
she notes that he is "white and ruddy, the chiefest among ten
thousand" (literally, both dazzling white and bloodred, the
leader of an innumerable host). This must apply in the fullest
sense only to the very God of creation, dwelling in impregna-
ble light and yet becoming a sacrificial Lamb to redeem His
beloved. He is both omnipotent God and dying Savior.

No wonder, after such a testimony, the daughters of Jerusalem exclaim in joy: "Whither is thy beloved gone?" May
God help us also to bear such a testimony!

Scripture:
Song of Solomon 5:9-16; 6:1; Acts 20:28;
Luke 4:22; Psalm 45:2

Hath God Said

Now the serpent…said unto the
woman, Yea, hath God said, Ye shall
not eat of every tree of the garden?

Satan constantly seeks to plant doubts about God's Word in our minds. And Eve's response in the garden demonstrates just how deceptive his lies can be. When faced with Satan's lies, Eve primarily failed to quote God's instructions accurately. She even added the words "neither shall ye touch it," which made God appear to be harsh in His demands. Uncertainty or ignorance of God's Word is the first step in falling for the lies of the enemy.

The wiles of Satan were not left in the chapters of Genesis, however. Paul warned the Corinthians to beware of the tactics Satan used on Eve in the Garden: "I fear, lest by any means, as the serpent beguiled Eve through his subtlety, so your minds should be corrupted from the simplicity that is in Christ." Temptation is ever present for all believers.

The answer is a renewed mind, keeping our thoughts focused on what God says is important: "Finally, brethren, whatsoever things are true, whatsoever things are honest, whatsoever things are just, whatsoever things are pure, whatsoever things are lovely, whatsoever things are of good report; if there be any virtue, and if there be any praise, think on these things."

Scripture:

Genesis 3:1; 2 Corinthians 11:3; Romans 12:2; Philippians 4:8

The Good Part

*But one thing is needful: and Mary
hath chosen that good part, which
shall not be taken away from her.*

Mary and Martha from Bethany both loved the Lord Jesus and wanted to please Him. Martha served through her activity, whereas Mary simply "sat at Jesus' feet, and heard his word." Jesus commented that Mary had rather chosen the "good part." It was something lasting that would "not be taken away from her."

The patriarch Job, whom God had said was "a perfect and an upright man" with "none like him in the earth," also chose what was good: "I have esteemed the words of his mouth more than my necessary food," Job said. Today we can sit at Jesus' feet every day when we read and meditate on His Word. Taking time for this "good part" must be a priority for every follower of the Lord. The psalmist wrote, "O how love I thy law! it is my meditation all the day."

We have a higher privilege than Job or the psalmist or even Mary, for we have *all* the Scriptures! If we truly desire "that good part," the Lord will surely provide the time, as He did for Mary.

Scripture:

Luke 10:39-42; Job 1:8; 23:12; Psalm 119:97

The Elect Lady

The elder unto the elect lady and her children,
whom I love in the truth; and not I only, but
also all they that have known the truth.

The Greek word for "lady" (*kuria*) is used only two times in the Bible, both in John's second letter. Interestingly, *kuria* is the feminine form of *kurios*, the Greek word translated "Lord." It is significant that this mother is called *kuria* instead of the much more frequently used *gune* ("woman") or even *meter* ("mother"). *Kuria* was evidently used to stress deep respect and honor to such a mother in the church.

She clearly was training her children in the truth, much as Timothy's mother, Eunice, and grandmother, Lois, had brought him up to have "unfeigned faith" in God's Word.

The second use of *kuria* is in verse 5: "I beseech thee, lady, not as though I wrote a new commandment unto thee, but that which we had from the beginning, that we love one another." Faith in the Lord and knowledge of His truth will ultimately be expressed through genuine love.

Scripture:
2 John; 2 Timothy 1:5; 3:15

Defining Faith

These all died in faith, not having received the
promises, but having seen them afar off, and
were persuaded of them, and embraced them.

How do we define faith and then appropriate it for our own lives? The Bible gives us examples of how faith is defined by God and demonstrated by His people. Elizabeth, the mother of John the Baptist, said of Mary, "Blessed is she that believed: for there shall be a performance of those things which were told her from the Lord."

Paul knew that God intended for him to go to Rome, so when his ship was about to sink, he encouraged his fellow travelers, "Be of good cheer: for I believe God, that it shall be even as it was told me." Abraham, Paul tells us, "staggered not at the promise of God through unbelief; but was strong in faith, giving glory to God; and being fully persuaded that, what he had promised, he was able also to perform." Sarah, who according to this promise conceived a child, "judged him faithful who had promised."

So what is biblical faith? It is a firm belief that God is both capable and faithful to perform what He has promised. This kind of faith brings the future into present reality.

Scripture:

Hebrews 11:11,13; Luke 1:45; Acts 27:25; Romans 4:20-21

The Prophet's Chamber

Let us make a little chamber...and
let us set for him there a bed, and a
table, and a stool, and a candlestick.

This sparsely furnished little room, built by the kindly Shunammite woman and her elderly husband, was the prototype of the so-called "prophet's chambers" that have been built for traveling preachers ever since. Little did this faithful couple anticipate how their kindness would bear fruit in the days to come.

In the first place, to show his appreciation, Elisha prayed that the Lord would give them a son, and God miraculously answered.

Tragically, the boy died quite suddenly several years later while Elisha was at Mount Carmel, some 15 miles away. The Shunammite woman laid her son on Elisha's bed in the prophet's chamber and then rode hastily to find Elisha. By the time the prophet arrived, the boy lay dead on his bed. But then Elisha prayed once again, and the dead child was restored to life.

The Shunammite mother and her son are never heard from again. And little do we think of that little room she made for Elisha, but her simple service for the Lord and His prophet has been an inspiration and example to multitudes.

Scripture:
2 Kings 4:9-10,16-17,33-35

An Inheritance in Our Father's House

Rachel and Leah answered and said unto him, Is there yet any portion or inheritance for us in our father's house?

This is the first mention of the word "inheritance" in the Bible, and appropriately enough, its theme is the futility of basing one's future plans on the hope of any earthly estate.

No earthly inheritance could ever be compared with "the riches of the glory of his inheritance in the saints." Of course, "children are an heritage of the LORD: and the fruit of the womb is his reward," and that's a promise for us on this earth.

So what is the nature of our real inheritance, then? It is called an "eternal inheritance," an "inheritance incorruptible, and undefiled," and a "glorious inheritance." The psalmist says, "The LORD is the portion of my inheritance."

We are sometimes better off with little or no earthly material inheritance, but when we are born again, we become "the children of God: and if children, then heirs; heirs of God, and joint-heirs with Christ." Thus, in Christ, the Lord also becomes the portion of our inheritance.

Scripture:
Genesis 31:14; Ephesians 1:18; Psalm 16:5; 127:3;
Hebrews 9:15; 1 Peter 1:4; Romans 8:16-17

Stricken in Years

*Zacharias said unto the angel, Whereby
shall I know this? for I am an old man,
and my wife well stricken in years.*

Seven people in the Bible are described as "stricken in years" or "stricken in age." Two of these are in the New Testament—Zacharias and Elizabeth, parents of John the Baptist.

This description was applied to Joshua four times and once to David, men called to key ministries in God's great plan. However, it was first applied to Abraham and Sarah, under circumstances remarkably similar to those of Zacharias and Elizabeth. "Now Abraham and Sarah were old and well stricken in age." Like Elizabeth, Sarah was barren and waiting on the Lord for a child, the promised heir Isaac.

These couples faced the same dilemma, and yet God promised them each a son who would become significant in fulfilling the plan of redemption for all mankind. With God, all things are possible.

These two amazing events assure us that God always fulfills His word, even when providential intervention is required. And regardless of how "stricken in years" we may be, He still has important work for us to do as long as we live.

Scripture:
Luke 1:18; Joshua 13:1; 23:1-2; 1 Kings 1:1; Genesis 18:11

A Divine Mission

Who knoweth whether thou art come to
the kingdom for such a time as this?

The great challenge to Queen Esther by her cousin Mordecai embodies a timeless principle that has challenged many other men and women of God in later times. Paul, for example, testified that "what things were gain to me, those I counted loss for Christ." God used him greatly in the formation of the early church.

Throughout church history, there have been men like Wycliffe and Hus and Luther and many others who, like Paul, could say, "Neither count I my life dear unto myself, so that I might finish my course with joy, and the ministry, which I have received of the Lord Jesus."

Who is to say that the same principle does not apply, at least in some measure, to all of us? Our role in history may not seem as strategic as that of Queen Esther, but God has a high calling or vital ministry for every one of His children.

May God help each of us, called just as we are to serve our Lord, to be able to say with Esther, "If I perish, I perish," and with Paul, "I have fought a good fight, I have finished my course, I have kept the faith."

Scripture:

Esther 4:14-16; Philippians 3:7; Acts 20:24; 2 Timothy 4:7

Handfuls of Purpose

*Let fall also some of the handfuls of
purpose for her, and leave them, that she
may glean them, and rebuke her not.*

This verse contains the unusual instruction of Boaz to his servants concerning Ruth, after she asked if she could glean after the reapers in his field of barley. Boaz not only allowed this but also commanded his servants to "let fall some of the handfuls of purpose" for her.

It is interesting that one Hebrew word, which means "take a spoil," is used twice in this verse, once translated "let fall" and once as "of purpose." The word for "handfuls," used only this once in the Bible, evidently refers to a hand's grip. This was a deliberate gift from Boaz, but Ruth was not to know so that she could assume she had gleaned it all on her own.

Boaz provided that which represented the bread of life as a gift to his coming bride. In this, as in other ways, Boaz is a type of Christ, and Ruth is a type of each believer destined for union with Him.

But the sheaves also represent God's Word, from which we glean life-giving food for our souls. Our heavenly "Boaz" has paid the price to take the spoil for us, but as we kneel down to glean each morsel, we can say, "I rejoice at thy word, as one that findeth great spoil."

Scripture:
Ruth 2:16; Psalm 119:162

The Golden Scepter

*The king held out to Esther the golden
scepter that was in his hand. So Esther drew
near, and touched the top of the scepter.*

Despite being the king's favorite wife, Queen Esther knew she was risking her life when she came into his presence without an invitation. But she also knew she had "come to the kingdom for such a time as this," and so she said, "If I perish, I perish." The king, however, extended his golden scepter to her and even said, "What is thy request? it shall be given thee."

In a beautiful way, this is also a picture of our own coming to Christ, the King of kings. How marvelous that "whosoever will" may come, whether queen or peasant. The Lord Jesus Christ graciously says to those who come to Him in faith, believing, "Whatsoever ye shall ask in my name, that will I do."

Esther was in a dilemma, but we are exhorted to "come boldly unto the throne of grace, that we may obtain mercy, and find grace to help in time of need." We have been called by our heavenly King, of whom God said, "A scepter of righteousness is the scepter of thy kingdom."

Scripture:
Esther 4:14,16; 5:2-6; Revelation 22:17;
John 14:13; Hebrews 1:8; 4:16

77

Justified by Faith and Works

Ye see then how that by works a man
is justified, and not by faith only.

James is referring to Genesis 15:6, which contains the first mention of faith in the Bible, here giving the example of Abraham. Paul stated clearly in Romans, "Being justified by faith, we have peace with God through our Lord Jesus Christ."

Yet James said a man is justified by works! How can both be true? The answer is that genuine saving faith necessarily produces works that demonstrate the reality of that faith.

It is significant that James speaks of Abraham's works as being a "fulfillment" of the Scripture. The testimony in Genesis that Abraham's faith was counted as righteousness was thus, in effect, a prophecy! Abraham obeyed God because he believed God! This is the obedience of faith.

Thus, a person is justified before God by his faith and justified before men by his works. God looks on the heart, but the world must look on the life. Abraham could not even know that his own faith was genuine until it was tested in the crucible of obedience, and the same is true for us today. A person is saved by grace "through faith...not of works," but that saving faith is "unto good works," and the one inevitably produces the other if it is real.

Scripture:
James 2:23-24; Romans 5:1; Ephesians 2:8-10

Casting Your Cares

…casting all your care upon
him; for he careth for you.

Paul reminds us in Philippians to "be careful for nothing; but in every thing by prayer and supplication with thanksgiving let your requests be made known unto God." There is a kind of care that is excessive to the point of distraction, as Martha exhibited. She was overcome by it, but Jesus corrected her: "Martha, Martha, thou art careful and troubled about many things."

This kind of care or anxiety is to be cast upon the Lord, because God cares for every one of His children. "When he saw the multitudes, he was moved with compassion on them, because they fainted, and were scattered abroad, as sheep having no shepherd."

The prodigal son knew what genuine care was. "When he was yet a great way off, his father saw him, and had compassion, and ran, and fell on his neck, and kissed him." Along with Paul's exhortation to "be careful for nothing," Jesus extends His everlasting compassion and gives us an invitation to cast our cares upon Him.

Scripture:
1 Peter 5:6-7; Philippians 4:6; Luke 10:41; 15:20;
Matthew 9:36

The Turning of the Day

*Then came the woman in the dawning of the
day, and fell down at the door of the man's
house where her lord was, till it was light.*

This tragic story took place in Israel in a time when "every man did that which was right in his own eyes." This woman, a concubine to a Levite, had been unfaithful to him, but he had taken her back. They were traveling to Ephraim, staying overnight in a city of Benjamin. However, the "sons of Belial" abused the woman throughout the night, leaving her dead at "the dawning of the day."

The whole sordid story illustrates the depths of depravity to which even God's chosen people can descend under cover of darkness.

There is an interesting scientific insight here that is often overlooked. The Hebrew word used for "dawning" (Hebrew, *panah*) is also the word for "turning." Rather than the rising of the sun, this refers to the rotation of the earth, which once again turns its face to the "light of the world."

There is, of course, a glorious dawning to come, when we shall dwell in the presence of the One who is the true light of the world, and "there shall be no night there."

Scripture:

Judges 19:26; 21:25; Ephesians 5:11-12; Revelation 21:25

Michal and David

Michal let David down through a window:
and he went, and fled, and escaped.

David's first wife, Michal, was an enigmatic and somewhat pathetic young woman. She loved David at first, but she eventually "despised him in her heart." What changed her attitude?

Initially, Michal was attracted to David on the basis of his military exploits and for other physical reasons, not because of his character or his love for God. Even when she helped him escape from her father, she used an "image"—a household idol—made up to look like David in his bed. Michal professed to worship the true God of Israel, but she had compromised her faith and worshipped other gods. When David lived in exile, she actually married another man, at her father's instigation. David later forced her return.

But her final rejection came as she mocked David's display of joy at the return of the ark of the covenant. It's clear she loved neither God nor her husband any longer.

What a sad end for a king's daughter! And what a warning her life becomes to compromising Christians, both to those who marry purely because of physical love and also to those who cling to the religious philosophies and practices of the world.

Scripture:
1 Samuel 18:20; 19:12-13; 25:44; 2 Samuel 3:13-16; 6:12-23

Love, Faith, Joy

*...whom having not seen, ye love; in
whom, though now ye see him not, yet
believing, ye rejoice with joy unspeakable.*

Peter's encouragement to the scattered believers reminds us
that in the midst of trials, we can still have love, faith, and
joy, even without ever having seen Jesus. The Lord Jesus Himself declared, "Blessed are they that have not seen, and yet have
believed." How did these persecuted Christians respond to
Jesus in their trials?

They loved Him. Love makes a trial bearable. "Who shall
separate us from the love of Christ? shall tribulation, or dis-
tress, or persecution, or famine, or nakedness, or peril, or
sword?" He loves us too much to abandon us, and we love
Him in return.

They believed. "Thou wilt keep him in perfect peace, whose
mind is stayed on thee: because he trusteth in thee." The
prophet Jeremiah wrote, "Blessed is the man that trusteth in the
LORD, and whose hope the LORD is." Our faith is well founded.

They rejoiced. "Rejoice, inasmuch as ye are partakers of
Christ's sufferings; that, when his glory shall be revealed, ye
may be glad also with exceeding joy." The proper response to
trials brings inexpressible joy.

Scripture:
1 Peter 1:7-9; 4:13; John 20:29; Romans 8:35;
Isaiah 26:3; Jeremiah 17:7-8

Rest and Work

*Come unto me, all ye that labor and are
heavy laden, and I will give you rest.*

Burdens come in all shapes and sizes—sorrow, pain, grief, fear, worry, and of course, sin. Jesus promises hope for the "heavy laden" if we will but come to Him. He will remove the burden, lighten it, or give us strength to bear it—whichever is best. The rest He provides includes inner peace here, even in times of trouble, and perfect peace hereafter.

Even though we are children of the King, we still have work to do. It has always been so, for even sinless Adam and Eve were responsible for tending the garden of Eden. God knew that idleness and lack of responsibility were improper. Likewise, in the future, we will be given responsibilities according to the handling of our responsibilities in this life. We may someday be co-regents of the kingdom, but we will still have our responsibilities.

The burdens God gives us now are not oppressive, but with His help, and with the proper attitude, His yoke is easy, and His burden is light.

Scripture:

Matthew 11:28-29; 25:21; Genesis 2:15; Revelation 20:6

The Strength of the Lord

I will go in the strength of the Lord GOD.

God the Creator is omnipotent, so we can accomplish much if we "go in the strength of the Lord GOD." The book of Psalms testifies again and again that God is indeed our strength. "I will love thee, O LORD, my strength. The LORD is my rock, and my fortress, and my deliverer; my God, my strength, in whom I will trust." But how do we appropriate God's strength?

Through reverence. "The LORD taketh pleasure in them that fear him, in those that hope in his mercy."

Through the Spirit. "Not by might, nor by power, but by my Spirit, saith the LORD of hosts."

Through joy. "The joy of the LORD is your strength."

Through weakness. "My strength is made perfect in weakness."

God promises, "Fear thou not; for I am with thee: be not dismayed; for I am thy God: I will strengthen thee; yea, I will help thee; yea, I will uphold thee with the right hand of my righteousness."

Scripture:

Psalm 71:16; 18:1-2; 147:10-11; Zechariah 4:6; Nehemiah 8:10;
2 Corinthians 12:9; Isaiah 41:10

Our Merciful God

It is of the LORD's mercies that we are not
consumed, because his compassions fail not. They
are new every morning: great is thy faithfulness.

God is merciful, not merciless. He is compassionate, not
hard-hearted. He is loving, not cruel. He is kind, not
pitiless.

Salvation is a marvelous display of His mercy. "God, who
is rich in mercy, for his great love wherewith he loved us, even
when we were dead in sins, hath quickened us together with
Christ." In fact, without God's mercies there is no hope. "It is
of the LORD's mercies that we are not consumed."

Of course, mercy is not receiving what we deserve, which
is eternal punishment. Instead, it answers the prayer of the
humble sinner, "God be merciful to me a sinner," who finds
that "the LORD is merciful and gracious, slow to anger, and
plenteous in mercy." God's mercy is all-encompassing. "He
that trusteth in the LORD, mercy shall compass him about." It
is also unfailing. "The mercy of the LORD is from everlasting
to everlasting upon them that fear him."

Scripture:
Lamentations 3:22-23,31-32; Ephesians 2:4-5;
Luke 18:13; Psalm 103:8-11,17; 32:10

Joy in Believing

Though now ye see him not, yet believing, ye
rejoice with joy unspeakable and full of glory.

After His resurrection, the Lord honored the request of His doubting disciple, Thomas, to see for himself that He had, indeed, returned from the grave. Then Jesus gave him a loving rebuke: "Thomas, because thou hast seen me, thou hast believed: blessed are they that have not seen, and yet have believed."

Jesus was not asking Thomas to exercise blind faith. Today we have an abundance of evidence, more even than the disciples themselves had, and there is no excuse not to believe. "For we are saved by hope: but hope that is seen is not hope: for what a man seeth, why doth he yet hope for? But if we hope for that we see not, then do we with patience wait for it."

We cannot yet see Him with our eyes, but we see Him by faith. We see Him on the cross, taking "our sins in his own body." We see the empty tomb and are like John, who "saw, and believed." Then we "rejoice with joy," looking forward to the day we shall see Him in His glory. For "when he shall appear, we shall be like him; for we shall see him as he is."

Scripture:
1 Peter 1:8; 2:24; John 20:8,29; Romans 8:24-25; 1 John 3:2

The Power and Fruit of the Spirit

*The fruit of the Spirit is love, joy, peace,
longsuffering, gentleness, goodness, faith, meekness,
temperance: against such there is no law.*

The power of the Holy Spirit for witnessing may well be essentially the fruit of the Spirit. Note how power is associated with the ninefold fruit of the Spirit.

- *Love.* "God hath not given us the spirit of fear; but of power, and of love."

- *Joy and peace.* "Now the God of hope fill you with all joy and peace in believing, that ye may abound in hope, through the power of the Holy Ghost."

- *Longsuffering and gentleness.* "By pureness, by knowledge, by longsuffering, by kindness…by the power of God."

- *Goodness.* "Now the God of hope fill you…through the power of the Holy Ghost…that ye also are full of goodness."

- *Faith.* "My speech and my preaching was…in demonstration of the Spirit and of power: that your faith should not stand in the wisdom of men, but in the power of God."

- *Meekness.* "For the kingdom of God is not in word, but in power…In the spirit of meekness."

- *Temperance.* The idea of temperance is, basically, that of a disciplined mind. God's gift is "the spirit of power, and of love, and of a sound mind."

Scripture:

Galatians 5:22-23; 2 Timothy 1:7; Romans 15:13-14;
1 Corinthians 2:4-5; 4:20-21; 2 Corinthians 6:6

Walking in Truth

*I have no greater joy than to hear
that my children walk in truth.*

The important word "truth" is a key word in the apostle John's vocabulary, occurring more in his writings than in those of any other New Testament author. In the one-chapter letter of 3 John, it occurs six times.

He addressed his letter to "Gaius, whom I love in the truth." He rejoiced over "the truth that is in thee." He urged his readers to be "fellowhelpers to the truth" and commended Demetrius, who had a good report "of the truth itself."

Every godly Christian parent or pastor knows exactly how John felt. There is no greater joy to such mature believers than to know that their children—whether physical or spiritual children—are growing in Christian faith and practice, walking in the truth.

John's very first mention of truth was in relation to Jesus Christ, whose glory he had beheld in His incarnation, as "full of grace and truth." In fact, Christ Himself claimed, "I am the truth." Then He also said, "Thy word is truth."

To walk in the truth, bringing joy to the Father, is to believe on Christ and then to trust and obey His Word as taught by the witnessing Spirit.

Scripture:
3 John; John 1:14; 14:6; 17:17

The Presence of the Lord

Glory and honor are in his presence;
strength and gladness are in his place.

Every believer is, in a real sense, perpetually in God's presence. Our bodies are the temples of the Holy Spirit—we can go nowhere without Him. Wherever we are or whatever we're facing, He is with us, and we can speak to Him about anything, anytime.

And as we are with Him, we are also continually in the presence of "glory and honor" and "strength and gladness." The psalmist says, "In thy presence is fullness of joy; at thy right hand there are pleasures for evermore."

Of course, we do not yet see Him face-to-face. But that day is coming too, for He "is able to keep you from falling, and to present you faultless before the presence of his glory with exceeding joy." There will be exceeding joy at His right hand, in His presence.

But, sadly, those who reject Him will know neither His presence now nor His presence in glory. All those who "know not God, and that obey not the gospel...shall be punished with everlasting destruction from the presence of the Lord, and from the glory of His power."

Scripture:
1 Chronicles 16:27; 1 Corinthians 6:19; Psalm 16:11;
Jude 24; 2 Thessalonians 1:8-9

Precious to the Lord

*Precious in the sight of the LORD
is the death of his saints.*

E ver since Eden, death has been mankind's greatest enemy. Despite our efforts to stall the inevitable, the normal life span continues to be 70 to 80 years, just as it was in the days of Moses.

What was the cause of death? "Sin, when it is finished, bringeth forth death." However, Christ died for our sins, "that through death he might destroy him that had the power of death."

And although death is still the great enemy, those who have been redeemed and forgiven through faith in Christ no longer need to fear "the sting of death," for "while we were yet sinners, Christ died for us."

We can rejoice because when a true Christian dies, the Lord Himself has called him home, and the death of one of His saints is indeed precious in His sight.

We should especially thank God for those Christians who have given their lives in defending the faith, preserving our freedom to worship and serve the Lord without fear.

Scripture:
Psalm 116:15; 90:10; James 1:15; Hebrews 2:14;
1 Corinthians 15:56; Romans 5:8

Joy in the Morning

*His anger endureth but a moment; in his
favor is life: weeping may endure for a
night, but joy cometh in the morning.*

God is holy and cannot ignore human sin, so His righteous anger is necessary because He is a just God. Nevertheless, He is also a God of love. His very purpose in creation was that His love could be demonstrated to men and women created in His image.

Sin has, of course, brought suffering and death, but still He is "slow to anger, and plenteous in mercy." He has provided salvation to all who will accept it, through the substitutionary death of His Son, who "for the joy that was set before him endured the cross, despising the shame, and is set down at the right hand of the throne of God."

All of us endure pain and weeping, but as measured in the scales of eternity, these will only "endure for a night." In heaven, "God shall wipe away all tears from their eyes; and there shall be no more death, neither sorrow, nor crying, neither shall there be any more pain."

Paul said that "our light affliction, which is but for a moment, worketh for us a far more exceeding and eternal weight of glory."

Scripture:

Psalm 30:5; 103:8; Hebrews 12:2; Revelation 21:4;
2 Corinthians 4:17

Love or Lust

*My son, attend unto my wisdom, and bow thine
ear to my understanding: that thou mayest regard
discretion, and that thy lips may keep knowledge.*

In the beginning, God created man and woman to come
together in holy union to make another human being. And
here in Proverbs 5, Solomon is teaching his son about that
sacred right reserved for married couples.

Verses 3 through 6 provide insight into the character of
promiscuity, which includes deception and sorrow. The solu-
tion, of course, is to stay away. Don't play with fire! Avoid any
opportunities to be enticed. The results of yielding to temptation include the loss of our youthful vigor, our wealth, our
health, our self-esteem, and even our lives. On the other hand,
married love provides health, companionship, joy, and sat-
isfaction. "Let thy fountain be blessed: and rejoice with the
wife of thy youth."

Remember, none of this is done in secret. "The ways of
man are before the eyes of the LORD, and he pondereth all
his goings." We should stay away from any involvement in
sin, for sin entraps us, and we keep going back. Men die for
lack of instruction or lack of obedience to the instruction they
have. This leads to great folly, and in the end, total shame and
destruction.

Scripture:
Proverbs 5

Abounding

*The law entered, that the offense might
abound. But where sin abounded,
grace did much more abound.*

Abounding sin is overcome by superabundant grace. No
matter how much sin has accumulated in a person's life,
God's grace found in Jesus Christ has the power to save, forgive, and blot out that sin. Once the believer has received the
Lord's grace, he can then abound…

In love toward others. "The charity of every one of you all
toward each other aboundeth."

In steadfast hope. "Now the God of hope fill you with
all joy and peace in believing, that ye may abound in hope,
through the power of the Holy Ghost."

In bringing forth fruit. "For if these things be in you, and
abound, they make you that ye shall neither be barren nor
unfruitful in the knowledge of our Lord Jesus Christ."

In thanksgiving. "Rooted and built up in him, and stab-
lished in the faith, as ye have been taught, abounding therein
with thanksgiving."

In God's work. "Therefore…be ye steadfast, unmovable,
always abounding in the work of the Lord, forasmuch as ye
know that your labor is not in vain in the Lord."

Scripture:

Romans 5:20; 15:13; 2 Thessalonians 1:3; Philippians 1:9;
2 Peter 1:8; Colossians 2:7; 1 Corinthians 15:58

Fear of Witnessing

And they called them, and commanded them not
to speak at all nor teach in the name of Jesus.

Why are most of us reluctant to witness to others? Fear. But in the face of fear, the apostles courageously answered that they "ought to obey God rather than men," and they prayed, "Lord, behold their threatenings: and grant unto thy servants, that with all boldness they may speak thy word."

But today we fear ridicule more than physical harm. Such fear is out of character for real Christians, "for God hath not given us the spirit of fear; but of power, and of love, and of a sound mind." If we love the Lord and those He died for, we must learn to conquer our fear of men.

But some, because of their high position, refused to take an open stand for Christ. "Among the chief rulers also many believed on him; but because of the Pharisees they did not confess him, lest they should be put out of the synagogue: for they loved the praise of men more than the praise of God."

May God give us the courage of Paul. "I am not ashamed of the gospel of Christ," he wrote, "for it is the power of God unto salvation to every one that believeth."

Scripture:
Acts 4:18,29; 5:29; 2 Timothy 1:7; John 12:42-43;
Romans 1:16

Marriage and Food:
Two Good Things

...forbidding to marry, and commanding
to abstain from meats, which God hath
created to be received with thanksgiving.

Paul knew that "in the latter times some shall depart from the faith, giving heed to seducing spirits, and doctrines of devils." The message could not be ignored, for Paul had received it from the Holy Spirit, who had spoken "expressly" on these matters. In addition to "speaking lies in hypocrisy; having their conscience seared with a hot iron," these false teachers make a false show of self-denial, "forbidding to marry, and commanding to abstain from meats."

Both cases, however, deny the clear teaching of Scripture, for both were created by God for His glory and our proper use, and are intrinsically good. Marriage was one facet of God's "very good" design. "Marriage is honorable in all, and the bed undefiled." Furthermore, He created food to provide nourishment for mankind. Everything He created is good if "received with thanksgiving" and "sanctified by the word of God and prayer."

Vows at a wedding and a word of thanks before meals—with these we can enjoy Him, His creation, and His provision.

Scripture:
1 Timothy 4:1-5; Genesis 1:28-29; 2:16-18,24; 9:3;
Hebrews 13:4

Fear Not

The angel said unto her, Fear not, Mary:
for thou hast found favor with God.

God knows just how crippling the emotion of fear can be for us. Many have been devastated by fear and have become slaves to it. In the Christmas narratives, there are several "fear not's."

The "fear not" of salvation. "And the angel said unto them, Fear not: for, behold, I bring you good tidings…which shall be to all people."

The "fear not" of the humanly impossible. "Fear not, Mary… the Holy Ghost shall come upon thee, and the power of the Highest shall overshadow thee…For with God nothing shall be impossible."

The "fear not" of unanswered prayer. "Fear not, Zacharias: for thy prayer is heard; and thy wife Elisabeth shall bear thee a son, and thou shalt call his name John."

The "fear not" of immediate obedience. "Joseph, thou son of David, fear not to take unto thee Mary thy wife."

Scripture reminds us, "There is no fear in love; but perfect love casteth out fear…He that feareth is not made perfect in love."

Scripture:
Luke 1:13,30,35,37; 2:10-11; 1 John 4:18-19;
Matthew 1:20,24

Fear Not, Little Flock

Seek ye the kingdom of God; and all
these things shall be added unto you.

Jesus was teaching His disciples not to be troubled over temporal things, but to rest in the fact that He will supply our needs. "If then God so clothe the grass…how much more will he clothe you?" We are not to have our mind set on material things, neither are we to be "of doubtful mind," wavering between hope and fear of the future.

The "nations of the world seek after" the things of the world. Our Father knows that we have need of certain things, and He loves us and has our best interests at heart, so we have nothing to fear.

It is not enough simply to stop fixating on the things of the world. We are to seek "the kingdom of God," to be about His business. His priorities should be our priorities. If they are, He will take pleasure in supplying our physical needs. In fact, Jesus tells us, "It is your Father's good pleasure to give you the kingdom."

It is our privilege to participate in His work on earth as He enables, "for where your treasure is, there will your heart be also."

Scripture:
Luke 12:22-34

Love in Action

Charity suffereth long, and is kind; charity envieth not; charity vaunteth not itself, is not puffed up.

In this famous "love chapter," Paul used the Greek word *agape*, which is translated "love" three times as often as it is translated "charity." Love is described not with adjectives or adverbs, but with verbs, with actions. "Charity" meant *agape* love—an unselfish, enduring, and active concern for others.

This passage lists 17 actions that love *does* or *does not* engage in. Love acts with patience and kindness; it does not envy others or seek to impress others, neither does it exhibit arrogance or conceit. Love is never rude, does not seek its own way, is slow to take offense, and bears no malice or resentment. Love does not gloat over the sins of others and is delighted when truth prevails. Love will bear up under any trial and will never lose faith; it is always hopeful and unlimited in its endurance.

This classic passage could in fact be read as a beautiful description of the Lord Jesus Christ Himself. That is, "Christ suffereth long, and is kind," and so on, finally climaxing in the great truth, "Christ never faileth." Jesus Christ is, indeed, love in action!

Scripture:
1 Corinthians 13

Sentimental Love for Jesus

He that hath my commandments, and
keepeth them, he it is that loveth me.

A large portion of Christian music today merely expresses subjective sentimentality with very little biblical content or practical application. It is proper for Christians to love the Lord Jesus Christ, of course, and to sing of that love. This love, however, is demonstrated by action. The one who really loves Him learns His commandments and obeys them. "If a man love me," Jesus says, "he will keep my words."

On the other hand, "He that loveth me not keepeth not my sayings." In these verses, the verb "keep" actually means "guard" as well as "obey," so the test of love also includes defending God's Word against its enemies. Christians offer various excuses when they fail to keep His Word—but the real reason is usually fear. However, even fear itself is inconsistent with love for Christ. "Herein is our love made perfect, that we may have boldness in the day of judgment…There is no fear in love; but perfect love casteth out fear: because fear hath torment. He that feareth is not made perfect in love. We love him, because he first loved us."

Scripture:
John 14:21-24; 1 John 4:17-19

Fullness of Blessing

*I am sure that, when I come unto you, I shall come
in the fullness of the blessing of the gospel of Christ.*

One beautiful characteristic of life in Christ is its fullness. Jesus Christ is Himself "the fullness of him that filleth all in all."

First of all, He gives fullness of grace. "And of his fullness have all we received, and grace for grace." Then comes fullness of joy and peace: "These things have I spoken unto you, that my joy might remain in you, and that your joy might be full."

We are commanded to "be filled with the Spirit." Not only does the Holy Spirit indwell us, but so do the Father and the Son, by the Spirit. Jesus said, "If a man love me, he will keep my words: and my Father will love him, and we will come unto him, and make our abode with him."

In Jesus Christ "dwelleth all the fullness of the Godhead bodily. And ye are complete in him." With the resources of such fullness of blessing available to us, we should be constantly growing "unto the measure of the stature of the fullness of Christ."

Scripture:

Romans 15:29; Ephesians 1:23; 4:13; 5:18;
John 1:16; 14:23; 15:11; Colossians 2:9-10

The Joy of the Lord

This day is holy unto our Lord: neither be ye
sorry; for the joy of the LORD is your strength.

Jerusalem's wall had been completed, God's Word had been
honored, and there was a great day of rejoicing. The real
joy in the hearts of the people, however, was not their joy—
it was the joy of the Lord. They rejoiced because He rejoiced,
and they shared His joy. The Lord rejoices when His love
is received and His purposes fulfilled. "He will save, he will
rejoice over thee with joy; he will rest in his love, he will joy
over thee with singing."

Redemption brings God joy. Therefore, Jesus, "for the joy
that was set before him endured the cross, despising the shame,
and is set down at the right hand of the throne of God." Joy
is in the Lord's heart whenever a believing sinner receives His
saving grace. That same joy is likewise experienced by each
believer whose testimony of life and word brings such a sinner to God.

Jesus said, "These things have I spoken unto you, that my
joy might remain in you, and that your joy might be full." His
joy is our joy, and the joy of the Lord is our strength.

Scripture:

Nehemiah 8:10; Zephaniah 3:17; Hebrews 12:2; John 15:11

Singing with the Hosts

They sing the song of Moses…saying, Great and
marvelous are thy works, Lord God Almighty;
just and true are thy ways, thou King of saints.

The fourth verse of the hymn "There's a Sweet and Blessed Story" speaks of the Christian hope, the ultimate realization of our full ransom.

> By and by with joy increasing
> And with gratitude unceasing,
> Lifted up with Christ forevermore to be;
> I will join the hosts there singing
> In the anthem ever ringing
> To the King of Love who ransomed me.

In this life we may go through a "fiery trial," but Peter encourages us, "Rejoice, inasmuch as ye are partakers of Christ's sufferings; that, when his glory shall be revealed, ye may be glad also with exceeding joy." We can always be "giving thanks unto the Father…who hath delivered [or ransomed] us from the power of darkness."

In the heavenly places, we will sing "a new song," a song of ransom. "Thou art worthy…for thou wast slain, and hast redeemed us to God by thy blood."

Scripture:
Revelation 5:9; 15:3; 1 Peter 4:12-13; Colossians 1:12-14

Christian Endurance

*Charity... beareth all things, believeth all
things, hopeth all things, endureth all things.*

The great "love" chapter in the Bible climaxes with the affirmation that *agape* love endures all things. Paul commands each of us to "endure hardness, as a good soldier of Jesus Christ." Looking especially to the last days, he tells Timothy, "Watch thou in all things, endure afflictions, do the work of an evangelist." James writes that blessing comes to the one who "endureth temptation: for when he is tried, he shall receive the crown of life." This speaks not merely of moral temptation, but of any testing in the Christian life.

We must also be willing to receive God's chastening. "For whom the Lord loveth he chasteneth...If ye endure chastening, God dealeth with you as with sons." In all this, Jesus Christ is our example and encouragement. "For consider him that endured such contradiction of sinners against himself, lest ye be wearied and faint in your minds."

Regardless of what God allows to come our way, He gives us strength to endure. The Lord Jesus, "for the joy that was set before him endured the cross," and so can we.

Scripture:
1 Corinthians 13:7; 2 Timothy 2:3; 4:5; James 1:12;
Hebrews 12:2-3,6-7

A Mighty Putdown

*He hath put down the mighty from their
seats, and exalted them of low degree.*

In the midst of Mary's song of praise to the Lord, she describes believers everywhere at various times during their lives. There are moments of great joy, as when Mary anticipated the birth of the baby Jesus, and then there are occasions of great turmoil and decision, such as persecution.

What is our hope when facing fiery circumstances? It is to remember "He that is mighty hath done to me great things; and holy is his name. And his mercy is on them that fear him from generation to generation."

Our verse declares that "He hath put down the mighty from their seats." Our dilemma is short lived, but his mercy goes on generation after generation.

Looking up from the depths of a defeat at the hands of oppressors, one wonders when will God exalt them of low degree. One answer is when we have exhausted our responsibilities, the rest is up to God, as He declares in Malachi: "Prove me now herewith, saith the LORD of hosts, if I will not open you the windows of heaven, and pour you out a blessing, that there shall not be room enough to receive it."

Scripture:
Luke 1:46-55; Malachi 3:10

I Will Remember
Thy Love for Me

*...that ye, being rooted and grounded
in love, may be able...to know the love
of Christ, which passeth knowledge.*

Christ's sacrificial love for us was remarkable. "Greater love hath no man than this, that a man lay down his life for his friends," which He did. "God commendeth his love toward us, in that, while we were yet sinners, Christ died for us."

The gospels give graphic portrayals of Christ's physical suffering on the cross, but a prophetic passage equally explicit is found in Isaiah, where we read that because of His treatment, "His visage was so marred more than any man." Why did He endure all this? "He was wounded for our transgressions, he was bruised for our iniquities...the LORD hath laid on him the iniquity of us all."

How should we react? Certainly by accepting His free gift of forgiveness, based on the truth that our sins are already paid for, but also with a heart of loving remembrance throughout our entire lives.

Scripture:

Ephesians 3:17-19; John 15:13; Romans 5:8;
Isaiah 52:14; 53:5-6

Children in Heaven

Who can tell whether GOD will be gracious to me,
that the child may live? But now he is dead…I
shall go to him, but he shall not return to me.

The death of a loved one is always a time of great sorrow, but the death of a child is perhaps the keenest sorrow of all. Nevertheless, for the Christian believer, we "sorrow not, even as others which have no hope."

Our text verse makes it clear that when a child dies (even one born of a sinful relationship, such as was this child of David and Bathsheba), that child goes to be with the Lord in heaven. Jesus said, "Suffer little children, and forbid them not, to come unto me: for of such is the kingdom of heaven."

Heaven is certainly a place where there are many little children. Although there are few specific Scriptures on this subject, what we do know, both from the love of God and the Word of God, suggests that the souls of all deceased little children are with the Lord in heaven, but also those who died in early childhood (and even before birth) from every time and place since the world began.

Scripture:
2 Samuel 12:22-23; 1 Thessalonians 4:13; Matthew 19:14

No Fear in the Days of Evil

Wherefore should I fear in the days of evil, when
the iniquity of my heels shall compass me about?

The "days of evil" seem specifically to refer to old age. Solomon reminds young people to "remember now thy Creator in the days of thy youth, while the evil days come not, nor the years draw nigh, when thou shalt say, I have no pleasure in them."

Those who have not "remembered their Creator" may one day come to realize that their iniquities actually involved the venom of that old serpent, the devil. Their sins might even destroy them both now and eternally. But because of Christ's great victory over Satan—when He both died for our sins and then defeated death by His resurrection—we need no longer fear death, even when the evil days are near.

Though it is far better to accept His gift of salvation from sin and death while we are young, it is never too late, as long as we live. So, "wherefore should I fear in the days of evil?" "We have known and believed the love that God hath to us. God is love; and...perfect love casteth out fear."

Scripture:

Psalm 49:5; Ecclesiastes 12:1; 1 John 4:16,18

The Dark Valleys

Though I walk through the valley
of the shadow of death…

There are many dark valleys mentioned in Scripture that typify the many sufferings and hard experiences through which we must pass. "For unto you it is given in the behalf of Christ, not only to believe on him, but also to suffer for his sake."

There is the vale of tears called Baca, or "weeping." Opinions differ as to whether this was an actual valley in Israel, but it came to symbolize a time of deep loss and sorrow. God's comfort will guide through Baca. "Blessed is the man whose strength is in thee…who passing through the valley of Baca… go from strength to strength."

Perhaps the darkest valley of all is the valley of the shadow of death, through which all must enter. For those without Christ, it is a valley of great fear. There have been multitudes "who through fear of death were all their lifetime subject to bondage."

But those who know the Lord need not fear, for God is with them. Even His guiding staff and buffeting rod are comforting, for they prove the love of the Shepherd. No wonder Psalm 23 is the most requested passage of Scripture by those deep in this dark valley.

Scripture:

Psalm 23:4; Philippians 1:29; Psalm 84:57; Hebrews 2:15

Bearing One Another's Burdens

*Bear ye one another's burdens, and
so fulfill the law of Christ.*

The word "burden" means a great weight, or load—something that is extremely hard to bear, or difficult to carry. The idea is that this kind of burden must be shared by another.

We should do all we can through intercessory prayer and witnessing, through compassionate ministry toward the infirm, showing mercy and love, and at times counting it a privilege to "weep with them that weep." Those who carry the burden of mental anguish and pressure need encouragement, not criticism. Bearing one another's burdens fulfills the law of Christ. This is not a law of legal obligation, but a law of love and grace. "My little children, let us not love in word, neither in tongue; but in deed and in truth."

There is a warning that "if a man think himself to be something, when he is nothing, he deceiveth himself." We should never feel so self-important, superior, or exclusive that we will not stoop to bear the heavy load of others. "Mind not high things, but condescend to men of low estate." One person who always bears our burdens is Christ. "Cast thy burden upon the LORD, and he shall sustain thee."

Scripture:
Galatians 6:2-3; Romans 12:15-16; 1 John 3:18;
Psalm 55:22; 1 Peter 5:7

Truth and Love

Speaking the truth in love…grow up into him
in all things, which is the head, even Christ.

Many Christians are sticklers for what they consider sound doctrine but are abrasive and unloving in their attitude toward those who hold other doctrines. Far more Christians, on the other hand, talk much about Christian love but consider doctrinal integrity of secondary significance—or worse.

The mature Christian, however, speaks the truth in love. That is, he understands, believes, and teaches the *truth* of God as revealed in His Word. At the same time, he does so in love, making "increase of the body unto the edifying of itself in love."

One cannot really *do* the truth or *teach* the truth without manifesting true love, nor can one manifest true love except in a context of genuine truth. "The fruit of the Spirit is love," and that Spirit who produces such fruit is "the Spirit of truth."

It is especially important not to be led away from sound biblical truth by teachers who downgrade doctrine in favor of what they may call love, for John exhorts us, "let us not love in word, neither in tongue; but in deed *and* in truth."

Scripture:

Ephesians 4:15-16; Galatians 5:22; John 15:26; 1 John 3:18

The Ransom Price

*The Son of man came...to give
his life a ransom for many.*

The thought that the death of Jesus was somehow the ransom price paid to redeem lost sinners from hell has been a stumbling block to many. Yet Scripture is clear. "Ye know that ye were not redeemed with corruptible things, as silver and gold...but with the precious blood of Christ."

In the Old Testament, ransoms were paid for various reasons, such as to free slaves. The last use of "ransom" in the Old Testament, however, seems to foreshadow the New Testament concept. "I will ransom them from the power of the grave; I will redeem them from death."

But to whom was the ransom of Christ to be paid? It can only have been paid to God Himself, for He had set "the wages of sin" to be death. Such a sacrifice was not foolishness, but "the power of God, and the wisdom of God."

"For there is one God, and one mediator between God and men, the man Christ Jesus; who gave himself a ransom for all, to be testified in due time."

Scripture:

Matthew 20:28; 1 Peter 1:18-19; Hosea 13:14; Romans 6:23;
1 Corinthians 1:24; 1 Timothy 2:5-6

The Christian's Lifestyle: Our Relationships

…submitting yourselves one to another in the fear of God.

Our calling is to walk worthy, our gifts are perfect and complete, and our behavior is changed by the new man. Our wisdom is to understand the will of the Lord, and our control is being filled with the Spirit.

Our relationships are to be carried out by submitting ourselves to one another in the fear of God. That key word, *hupotasso*, is instructive. It is a compound of the preposition "under" and a word that means "to arrange in order." Thus, "to arrange under, in order."

In the home, the submission (the order, or arrangement) is compared to the Lord's house, the church. Wives are to be arranged under the husband's authority just as the church is under the authority of Jesus Christ. Husbands are to be under the responsibility of sacrificial love just as Christ gave His life on behalf of and for the benefit of the church.

In the workplace, those who serve are to do so as though they were serving the Lord, not men. Those who lead are to relate to their servants as though they were serving the servants, recognizing that one Master is over all. These instructions are really quite simple. We do not need to complicate them.

Scripture:
Ephesians 5:21-33; 6:1-9

Good Gifts for Our Children

*If ye then, being evil, know how to give
good gifts unto your children, how much
more shall your Father which is in heaven
give good gifts to them that ask him?*

The Lord does not rebuke the giving of gifts to our children, especially when we give in such a way as to be a small picture of our heavenly Father giving gifts to His children. His gifts are always good gifts—gifts that are good for us, although they may not always seem so at first.

For example, "Unto you it is given in the behalf of Christ… to suffer for his sake." But when we suffer, "he giveth more grace." He may give a difficult day, but He also gives strength for the day. He may give an untraveled way, but then He gives light for the way.

"Every good gift and every perfect gift is from above, and cometh down from the Father of lights, with whom is no variableness, neither shadow of turning."

The apostle Paul reminds us of the greatest gift of all: "The gift of God is eternal life through Jesus Christ our Lord." And that is not all He gives! "He that spared not his own Son, but delivered him up for us all, how shall he not with him also freely give us all things?"

Scripture:
Matthew 7:11; Philippians 1:29; James 1:17; 4:6;
Romans 6:23; 8:32

Everlasting Love

I have loved thee with an everlasting love:
therefore with lovingkindness have I drawn thee.

God's love is an "everlasting love" and compels Him to act lovingly on our behalf. "Herein is love, not that we loved God, but that he loved us, and sent his Son to be the propitiation for our sins." We sing this theme in the grand hymn "I Am His, and He Is Mine."

> Loved with everlasting love, led by grace that love to know; / Spirit, breathing from above, Thou hast taught me it is so! / O this full and perfect peace! O this transport all divine! / In a love which cannot cease, I am His and He is mine.

Jesus prayed, "I in them, and thou in me…that the world may know that thou hast sent me, and hast loved them, as thou hast loved me." The Father will never allow us to part from Him or our Savior, who drew us to Himself in love.

"Behold, what manner of love the Father hath bestowed upon us, that we should be called the sons of God." In His grace, we come to Him, experiencing sweet forgiveness and everlasting love. Cradled in the security of His undying love, we have peace.

Scripture:
Jeremiah 31:3; 1 John 3:1; 4:10; John 17:23-24; Ephesians 1:4

Loving His Appearing

*...not to me only, but unto all them
also that love his appearing.*

The Lord has a special reward for all those who "love his appearing." The word "appearing" (Greek, *epiphaneia*) can refer to either the first or second advent of Christ, depending on the context. Paul urges us to be "looking for that blessed hope, and the glorious appearing of the great God and our Savior Jesus Christ."

At that great day of His second coming, "the Lord, the righteous judge" will award to those who have loved His appearing a special crown of righteousness, which must somehow be (as a wreath encircling the head of a victor in a race) an enveloping glow of divine appreciation for a godly life lived in daily anticipation of the Lord's return.

The apostle John beautifully expressed the way in which such a life, loving Christ's coming, produces a growing righteousness now and perfected righteousness then. "And now, little children, abide in him; that, when he shall appear, we may have confidence, and not be ashamed before him at his coming...We know that, when he shall appear, we shall be like him; for we shall see him as he is."

Scripture:
2 Timothy 4:8; Titus 2:13; 1 John 2:28; 3:2-3

Whom Shall I Fear

*The LORD is my light and my
salvation; whom shall I fear?*

David had more than his share of opposition—from family, from King Saul, from his generals, and even from his own son. If anyone had a need for deliverance, David did. He declared that his Lord was his light, salvation, and strength, and so He is to us.

The Lord is my *light*. When we walk in His light, we do not stumble. "Rejoice not against me, O mine enemy: when I fall, I shall arise; when I sit in darkness, the LORD shall be a light unto me."

The Lord is my *salvation*. God delivers His children from danger, including deliverance from the penalty of sin. "Help us, O God of our salvation, for the glory of thy name: and deliver us, and purge away our sins, for thy name's sake."

The Lord is the *strength of my life*. God is our defense, a place of refuge. "The LORD is my rock, and my fortress, and my deliverer; my God, my strength, in whom I will trust."

Even in the face of seemingly overwhelming opposition, we have no need to fear. Our focus should be on the source of deliverance rather than on the problem.

Scripture:
Psalm 27:1,14; 79:9; 18:2; Micah 7:8

The Fear of the Lord

Come, ye children, hearken unto me: I
will teach you the fear of the LORD.

This testimony of one who fears the Lord is contrasted with the destinies of those who don't. David explains what it means to fear the Lord and invites all who read to join him in fearing God.

The "fear of the LORD" is not so much an attitude as it is a life commitment. "What man is he that desireth life, and loveth many days, that he may see good?" A God-fearing man or woman desires a long life of ministry to others.

"Keep thy tongue from evil, and thy lips from speaking guile." We know that the tongue is capable of incredible harm. The one who fears the Lord should be characterized by a lifestyle of guarded speech.

We are to "depart from evil, and do good." Our life's motive should be to "seek peace, and pursue it." Attaining peace may not be easy, but we should strive for it.

As a result, our gracious Lord promises, "The angel of the LORD encampeth round about them that fear him, and delivereth them."

"O fear the LORD, ye his saints: for there is no want to them that fear him."

Scripture:

Psalm 34

Deliverance from Fear

…and deliver them who through fear of death were all their lifetime subject to bondage.

The Son of God took on our humanity "that through death he might destroy him that had the power of death, that is, the devil." Death is the wages of sin and the last enemy. Its "bondage" affects all of creation.

Some today consider death as a part of our Lord's original, "very good" creation. This is sad, for it impugns the very goodness of our Creator, who directs our attention even to the beauty of flowers and is concerned that we care for animals. Why, then, would He direct and superintend the death and destruction of billions of animals, unless it served to amplify His horror of man's sinful rebellion?

When Jesus eventually came, He "abolished death" and "brought life and immortality to light through the gospel." In the future, there shall be "no more death, neither sorrow, nor crying, neither shall there be any more pain: for the former things are passed away." Surely He hated death from the beginning.

Scripture:
Hebrews 2:14-15; 1 Corinthians 15:26; Romans 6:23; 8:21;
Genesis 1:31; Matthew 6:28-29; Proverbs 12:10;
2 Timothy 1:10; Revelation 21:4

Visible Love

My little children, let us not love in word,
neither in tongue; but in deed and in truth.

There is no doubt that God's people are to give alms to the poor and represent Christ even with a "cup of cold water" given in His name. But this passage emphasizes how the believer is to treat another Christian brother or sister, not the needy unbeliever.

John begins his letter by emphasizing that our fellowship is "in the light," producing love that is perfected by keeping God's Word, which in turn is necessary to abide in the light.

This commandment is as old as the beginning but also "new" in the sense that it now includes both Jew and Gentile.

The vivid example of love is clearly displayed by the substitutionary atonement of our Lord Jesus, whose selfless and sacrificial love demands both sympathy and empathy toward our brothers and sisters in Christ. It also demands specific action "in deed and in truth." Our precious Lord *felt* for us, but He also *did* for us.

The external action in addition to the internal attitude is certainly parallel to showing our faith by our works. We must be doers of the Word and not just hearers only.

Scripture:
1 John 1:7; 2:7-8; 3:18; Matthew 10:42; James 3:18; 1:22

His Everlasting Arms

The eternal God is thy refuge, and
underneath are the everlasting arms.

The third verse of the hymn "I Am His, and He Is Mine" testifies of the rest and peace we find in the "everlasting arms" of the Savior.

> Things that once were wild alarms cannot now disturb my rest; / Closed in everlasting arms, pillowed on the loving breast! / O to lie forever here, doubt and care and self resign, / While He whispers in my ear, I am His and He is mine.

The disciples cried out with alarm on a boat one evening when a storm arose. "Master, carest thou not that we perish?" Of course Jesus cared, for He loved them. So "he arose, and rebuked the wind, and said unto the sea, Peace, be still."

There was great friendship between Jesus and the disciple John. "Now there was leaning on Jesus' bosom one of his disciples, whom Jesus loved." A deep intimacy with Him can be ours if we will only pillow our head on Him.

Solomon uses the analogy of husband and wife to reflect the self-sacrificing love between our Lord and His children. "I am my beloved's, and my beloved is mine."

Scripture:
Deuteronomy 33:27; Mark 4:38; John 13:23;
Song of Solomon 6:3

Eternal Blessings

*Keep yourselves in the love of God, looking for the
mercy of our Lord Jesus Christ unto eternal life.*

We receive God's promise of life everlasting only
through faith in the person and work of Jesus Christ,
for "he that believeth on the Son hath everlasting life."

This is not just eternal existence—it is eternal blessing as well. We will have an eternal home and be joint heirs
with Christ. There will be eternal consolation and unending
glory for every believer, for God "hath called us unto his eternal glory." Therefore, "our light affliction, which is but for
a moment, worketh for us a far more exceeding and eternal
weight of glory."

These eternal blessings are all ours through Jesus Christ,
for He is "the author of eternal salvation" and has "obtained
eternal redemption for us," all accomplished through His own
shed "blood of the everlasting covenant."

We shall, in fact, reign as kings with Him in "the everlasting kingdom of our Lord and Savior Jesus Christ," where we
"shall reign for ever and ever." Best of all, however, we shall be
with our Savior throughout the endless ages to come.

Scripture:
Jude 21; John 3:36; 2 Corinthians 4:17; 5:1;
Hebrews 5:9; 9:12,15; 13:20; 1 Peter 5:10;
2 Peter 1:11; Revelation 22:5

God Remembers

God remembered Noah, and every living thing.

This is the first mention of the word "remember" in the Bible, and it tells us that God remembers! During the awful cataclysm of the Flood, the world's most devastating event, God remembered the faithful obedience of Noah, and He even remembered every living thing!

We may forget many things, but God remembers: "For God is not unrighteous to forget your work and labor of love, which ye have showed toward his name." Nor does He ever forget a promise. "Blessed be the Lord God of Israel; for he hath visited and redeemed his people...to remember his holy covenant; the oath which he sware to our father Abraham." That promise had been made 2000 years before, but God remembered.

God even remembers the sparrows: "Not one of them is forgotten before God." And He certainly remembers His own children: "He knoweth our frame; he remembereth that we are dust."

God remembers the evil as well as the good, of course. The one thing He chooses not to remember is the sinful past of those who have come to Christ for forgiveness: "Their sins and their iniquities will I remember no more."

Scripture:
Genesis 8:1; Hebrews 6:10; 8:12; 10:17;
Luke 1:68,72-73; 12:6; Psalm 103:14

Children of Light

Ye were sometimes darkness, but now are ye
light in the Lord: walk as children of light.

The Bible uses a number of beautiful metaphors to describe those who have become born again. As children tend to take on the characteristics of their parents, so God's spiritual children should "grow in grace, and in the knowledge of our Lord and Savior Jesus Christ."

Christians are called "the children of light, and the children of the day." Therefore, we should "walk as children of light." The Lord Jesus spoke of us as "children of the kingdom." We should therefore live and speak as those born into the kingdom of God and as faithful subjects of the King of kings.

Christ also called us children of wisdom, and this surely implies that we should have "the mind of Christ." In contrast, unbelievers are called "children of the wicked one."

"But if we walk in the light, as he is in the light," then we can no longer "walk in darkness," for we have "the light of life."

Scripture:
Ephesians 5:8; 2 Peter 3:18; 1 Thessalonians 5:5;
Matthew 13:38; 11:19; 1 Corinthians 2:16;
1 John 1:7; John 8:12

Preciousness

*Ye are…a peculiar people; that ye should show
forth the praises of him who hath called you
out of darkness into his marvelous light.*

Peter says our faith is "much more precious than…gold that perisheth." Why are we and our faith so special in God's sight?

Peter calls our Lord "a chief corner stone, elect, precious." Christ, in God's eyes, is precious. "This is my beloved Son, in whom I am well pleased." Why is He precious? For His purity, love, desire for God's will—all the ways in which we were *not* precious.

Christ, God's beloved Son, and His atoning blood are so precious to God that there is a limit to His patience toward those who reject Him. God will not allow His Son to be disallowed or disobeyed without penalty. Worthlessness is the state of those who reject, and judgment awaits them.

If we place our trust in Him, His preciousness is transferred to us. When God the Father looks at one who truly believes, He sees not only Christ's sinlessness but also His preciousness.

Scripture:
1 Peter 2:4-9; 1:7; 3:7; Matthew 3:17

Loving Others
As We Love Christ

*Inasmuch as ye have done it unto one of the least
of these my brethren, ye have done it unto me.*

This passage describes a time when the Lord shall hold
to account certain individuals who treated others who
were less privileged uncharitably, and He will bless those
who showed compassion and gave of themselves. Notice
that Christ takes such actions toward others as personal treatment of Himself. If we look with disdain upon a particular
believer—even the "least" one—that slight is personally felt
by our King.

Note James' warning about our words: "Therewith bless
we God, even the Father; and therewith curse we men, which
are made after the similitude of God." The closest analogy on
this earth to the God we love consists of the people around
us. They, not our favorite pet or cherished item, are made in
the image of God!

Christ told His disciples, "As the Father hath loved me,
so have I loved you: continue ye in my love." How has Christ
loved us? He loved us when we were sinners, rebels against His
will. If we are to continue in His love, we must love others as
we would love our precious Lord.

Scripture:
Matthew 25:37-40; James 3:9; John 15:9

Rejoicing Greatly

*...wherein ye greatly rejoice, though now
for a season, if need be, ye are in heaviness
through manifold temptations.*

Our lives are sometimes battered by various trials, or "manifold temptations," which are intended to bring about a pure and effective faith. Here Peter is summing up a list of blessings given in the preceding three verses, for which we can rejoice with him.

"*His abundant mercy.*" Mercy implies a compassionate act on one who is in desperate need. In context, God's mercy was granted to us in salvation when we could do nothing to save ourselves.

"*Begotten us again.*" We are now His children, born into His family. We now have spiritual and eternal life.

"*A lively hope.*" Not just a living hope—it is much more than that. We have a hope that is actively, vibrantly alive. Our eventual eternal resurrection is thus assured.

"*Kept by the power of God.*" The protection of God extends far beyond the inheritance; it encompasses the individual heir also—the one who has tasted of His mercy "through faith unto salvation."

Scripture:
1 Peter 1:3-6

Our God

Thy righteousness also, O God, is very
high, who hast done great things: O
God, who is like unto thee!

We cannot begin to know everything about God. On the
other hand, the Bible does speak about "that which
may be known of God."

He is "the God of hope," "the God of peace," "the God of
all comfort," and "the God of all grace." He is "rich in mercy,"
He "cannot lie," He is the "Judge of all," a "consuming fire."
His throne is forever, and the "worlds were framed" by Him.

"There is no power but of God," and "the foolishness of
God is wiser than men; and the weakness of God is stronger
than men." "There is none other God but one." He is not like
anything, but His creation reflects Him. All that is true and
wise and lovely is defined by His measure.

He alone is worthy of our praise. "Praise our God, all ye
his servants, and ye that fear him, both small and great."

Scripture:

Psalm 71:19; Romans 1:19; 13:1; 15:13,33; 1 Corinthians 1:25; 8:4;
2 Corinthians 1:3; Ephesians 2:4; Titus 1:2; Hebrews 1:8; 11:3;
12:23,29; 1 Peter 5:10; Revelation 19:5

The First Love

Thou lovedst me before the foundation of the world.

This is the very heart of the moving prayer of the Lord Jesus Christ in the upper room before His arrest and crucifixion. Then, after speaking of this love, Jesus prayed—in the final words of His sure-to-be-answered prayer—"that the love wherewith thou hast loved me may be in them, and I in them."

This love—the love within the Trinity—was the primeval love and therefore is the spring from which flows every other form of true love—marital love, mother love, brotherly love, love of country, love of friends, love for the lost, or any other genuine love.

It is appropriate that the first mention of love in the Old Testament refers to the love of a father (Abraham) for his son (Isaac), and that the first reference to love in the New Testament speaks of the heavenly love of God the Father for God the Son.

"He that spared not his own Son, but delivered him up for us all, how shall he not with him also freely give us all things?" One day, just as He prayed, we shall be with Him, see His glory, and even experience His own eternal love in our hearts.

Scripture:

John 17:24-26; Genesis 22:2; Matthew 3:17; Romans 8:32

Herein Is Love

Herein is love, not that we loved God,
but that he loved us, and sent his Son
to be the propitiation for our sins.

Biblical love is different from mere physical attraction and much more meaningful. It is significant that the Greek word for erotic love (*eros*) is never used in the Bible at all.

The original love—and therefore the source of all other love—was the eternal love within the triune Godhead. In the upper room Jesus prayed, "Father…thou lovedst me before the foundation of the world." He then prayed "that the love wherewith thou hast loved me may be in them."

We cannot fully comprehend the Father's love for the Son, for it is infinite, but love in terms of our human understanding is defined in our text. Herein is love: that God sent His own beloved Son to die for our sins. The biblical words for God's type of love (*agape*) occur 37 times in the 5 chapters of John's first epistle and 37 times in the 21 chapters of John's Gospel.

It is clear that the measure of true love is God's sacrificial love for us. Thus, as Jesus says, "Greater love hath no man than this, that a man lay down his life for his friends."

Scripture:
1 John 4:10-11; John 17:24; 15:13; 13:34

Disguises

He that hateth dissembleth with his lips,
and layeth up deceit within him; when
he speaketh fair, believe him not.

To "dissemble" is to hide under a false appearance in order to deceive and steal or destroy. Satan appeared to Eve as the beautiful serpent; Jacob disguised himself as Esau to obtain the birthright from his father; Rachel pretended the "custom of women" was upon her in order to keep her family's idols.

Disguises were also used to deceive others into fulfilling promises. Judah's widowed daughter-in-law, Tamar, disguised herself as a harlot and deceitfully kept Judah's bracelet and signet in order to assure her place in her husband's family. A prophet of the Lord disguised himself as a soldier wounded in battle in order to have the king pronounce judgment upon himself.

Where God is concerned, no man is able to disguise himself, for "all things are naked and opened unto the eyes of him." In our text verse, hatred intimates deception. Our calling is to love and to honestly share the truth of what makes us who we are—the grace of the Lord Jesus Christ.

Scripture:
Proverbs 26:24-25; Genesis 3; 27:23; 31:34-35; 38; 1 Kings
20:37-42; Hebrews 4:13

Grace and Mercy

*God, who is rich in mercy, for his great
love wherewith he loved us…*

Grace is receiving what we don't deserve, and mercy is *not* receiving what we *do* deserve. We don't deserve God's grace as evidenced in the sending of His Son to provide salvation.

Every spiritual blessing in Christ is undeserved; it is all of grace from beginning to end, "that in the ages to come he might show the exceeding riches of his grace in his kindness toward us through Christ Jesus. For by grace are ye saved through faith; and that not of yourselves: it is the gift of God."

What we do deserve is everlasting punishment and banishment from God. "But God, who is rich in mercy…made us sit together in heavenly places in Christ Jesus." "The Lord is merciful and gracious, slow to anger, and plenteous in mercy."

And just how merciful is He? "For as the heaven is high above the earth, so great is his mercy toward them that fear him."

"Surely goodness and mercy shall follow me all the days of my life: and I will dwell in the house of the Lord for ever."

Scripture:

Ephesians 2:4-8; Psalm 103:8,11; 23:6

Crown Him the Lord of Love

I am persuaded, that neither death, nor life, nor
angels, nor principalities, nor powers, nor things
present, nor things to come, nor height, nor depth, nor
any other creature, shall be able to separate us from
the love of God, which is in Christ Jesus our Lord.

God's great love for us moved Him to extend His grace to us. This love was not a sentimental, "feel good" love, but was sacrificial on our behalf. "Greater love hath no man than this, that a man lay down his life for his friends."

Soon after Christ rose from the dead, He appeared to His disciples. But doubting Thomas was not present, and he demanded to see proof before he believed. Several days later Jesus reappeared and removed all stumbling blocks to faith. "Reach hither thy finger, and behold my hands; and reach hither thy hand, and thrust it into my side: and be not faithless, but believing. And Thomas answered and said unto him, My Lord and my God." One day all the world will see those yet-visible wounds, for "they shall look upon [Christ] whom they have pierced."

Our Redeemer deserves all praise from redeemed sinners, "that God in all things may be glorified through Jesus Christ, to whom be praise and dominion for ever and ever."

Scripture:
Romans 3:23-24; 8:38-39; John 15:13; 20:27-28; 1 Peter 4:11

Jesus Touched Them

Jesus put forth his hand, and touched him.

This is the first occurrence in the New Testament of the word "touch," and here it was Jesus who was doing the touching. Jesus could merely speak a word to heal, as He did for the nobleman's son in Capernaum, who was healed from six miles away.

Often, however, He showed His love and concern by actually touching individuals even when they had contagious diseases, such as leprosy. On one occasion, a young man had actually died, but Jesus "came and touched the bier," and the dead man was raised from the dead.

Peter's mother-in-law was "sick of a fever," but Jesus "touched her hand, and the fever left her." On at least two occasions, blind men beseeched Him for their sight. "Then touched he their eyes…And their eyes were opened." When Peter impetuously cut off the ear of one of the soldiers sent to arrest Jesus, "he touched his ear, and healed him."

One touching was different. "They brought young children to him, that he should touch them." And despite the disciples' objections, "he took them up in his arms, put his hands upon them, and blessed them."

Scripture:
Matthew 8:3,14-15; 9:29-30; John 4:46-53;
Luke 7:14; 22:51; Mark 10:13,16

The Better Hope

*The law made nothing perfect, but the
bringing in of a better hope did; by the
which we draw nigh unto God.*

Men and women have many false hopes in this world, one
of which is that they can earn heaven by good works.
There is a better hope, however: "Christ in you, the hope of
glory."

In addition to the "better hope" in our text, the New Testament uses three other adjectives to describe our Christian
hope.

First, it is called a "good hope." "Now our Lord Jesus
Christ himself, and God, even our Father…hath loved us, and
hath given us everlasting consolation and good hope through
grace."

Next, it is a "blessed hope." "Denying ungodliness and
worldly lusts, we should live soberly, righteously, and godly, in
this present world; looking for that blessed hope, and the glorious appearing of the great God and our Savior Jesus Christ."

Finally, it is a "lively hope." "Blessed be the God and
Father of our Lord Jesus Christ, which according to his abundant mercy hath begotten us again unto a lively hope by the
resurrection of Jesus Christ from the dead."

Scripture:
Hebrews 7:19; Colossians 1:27; 2 Thessalonians 2:16;
Titus 2:12-13; 1 Peter 1:3

In Love

…with all lowliness and meekness, with
longsuffering, forbearing one another in love.

The beautiful little phrase "in love" (Greek, *en agape*) occurs
six times in Ephesians.

First of all, God "hath chosen us in [Christ] before the
foundation of the world, that we should be holy and without
blame before him in love." Our very position in Christ is centered in His love. This means that our spiritual lives are "rooted
and grounded in love" because of Him who is incarnate love.

This love of Christ for us must then display itself through
our lives. As our text urges, we must forbear one another in
love, regardless of the personal provocation.

In our witnessing and teaching, we must always be careful to be "speaking the truth in love" that the whole body of
Christ "may grow up into him in all things." This practice
"maketh increase of the body unto the edifying of itself in love."

Finally, we are to "walk in love, as Christ also hath loved
us." He has chosen us in love, rooted and grounded us in love,
and now we should forbear each other and build each other
up in love, speak the truth in love, and walk daily in His love.

Scripture:
Ephesians 1:4; 3:17; 4:2,15-16; 5:2

Megastorm, Megacalm, Megafear

He said unto them, Why are ye so fearful?
how is it that ye have no faith?

Life's pressures sometimes cause us to feel an intense fear. Christ desires to use these circumstances to develop in us an intense faith.

The disciples found themselves in a sudden, intense storm on the Sea of Galilee. Many of the disciples were experienced fishermen, quite familiar with this lake and its sudden, violent storms. But this storm was a "great [Greek, *megas*] storm," and the ship was filled with water.

There were two possible reactions: peace or panic. Despite the fact that they had seen Jesus' miracles for some two years, they panicked rather than resting in the peace of God.

When they awoke Jesus, the eternal Creator, fearful they were about to perish, the Lord simply arose and rebuked the wind: "Peace, be still." And the "great calm" (*mega*calm) prevailed, the waves were immediately still, the wind was intensely quiet, and the disciples "feared exceedingly." Or better, *mega*-fear possessed them.

As Christ lay back down to sleep, He spoke the words in our text, and He speaks them to us today. And our response should be, "Lord, I believe; help thou mine unbelief."

Scripture:
Mark 4:37-41; 9:24

136

Faith Turned to Sight

*The trial of your faith... might be found
unto praise and honor and glory at
the appearing of Jesus Christ.*

Since "we walk by faith, not by sight" in this life, with much
we don't yet understand, the prayer of each faithful saint
has mirrored John's response to the Lord's promise: "Even so,
come, Lord Jesus." The climactic verse of "It Is Well with My
Soul" focuses on this coming event.

> And Lord, haste the day when my faith shall
> be sight, / The clouds be rolled back as a scroll: /
> The trump shall resound, and the Lord shall
> descend, / Even so, it is well with my soul.

For centuries, faithful men and women have gazed
upward, desiring to see "the heaven departed as a scroll when it
is rolled together" at His return. As the great day draws nearer,
we should be all the more expectant. On that day, "the Lord
himself shall descend from heaven with a shout, with the voice
of the archangel, and with the trump of God: and the dead in
Christ shall rise first...Wherefore comfort one another with
these words." Until then, "it is well with my soul."

Scripture:
1 Peter 1:7-8; 2 Corinthians 5:7; Revelation 22:20; 6:14;
1 Thessalonians 4:16-18

The Pillar and Ground
of the Truth

The house of God…is the church of the living
God, the pillar and ground of the truth.

Exactly what does a church look like? Paul uses three phrases to describe three aspects of a biblical church.

The house of God. The household of God consists of a family of believers where love controls and where He is honored. "Ye also, as lively stones, are built up a spiritual house, an holy priesthood, to offer up spiritual sacrifices, acceptable to God by Jesus Christ."

The church of the living God. The *ekklesia*, or "called-out ones," serve the living God. "The blood of Christ [shall]… purge your conscience from dead works to serve the living God."

The pillar and ground of the truth. A facade pillar of a building is not used for support, but rather for display by elevating or calling attention to something else. The ground provides the support. The church should function to support and display the whole truth in such a way that all men can see and believe it.

It should be a family of believers exhibiting brotherly love, individually and corporately serving the living God out of a pure conscience, defending the truth, and displaying it to the lost.

Scripture:
1 Timothy 3:14-15; 1 Peter 2:5; Hebrews 9:14

Seven "Three Sixteens"

*Unto the woman he said, I will greatly
multiply thy sorrow and thy conception.*

There are seven significant "three-sixteens" in the Bible.

Genesis 3:16—a divine judgment. "Unto the woman he said, I will greatly multiply thy sorrow and thy conception."

Malachi 3:16—a divine blessing. "They that feared the LORD spake often one to another: and the LORD hearkened, and heard it, and a book of remembrance was written."

First Timothy 3:16—a divine mystery. "Great is the mystery of godliness: God was manifest in the flesh, justified in the Spirit, seen of angels, preached unto the Gentiles, believed on in the world, received up into glory."

Second Timothy 3:16—a divine book. "All Scripture is given by inspiration of God."

Colossians 3:16—a divine worship. "Let the word of Christ dwell in you richly in all wisdom; teaching and admonishing one another in psalms and hymns and spiritual songs, singing with grace in your hearts to the Lord."

First Corinthians 3:16—a divine dwelling. "Know ye not that ye are the temple of God, and that the Spirit of God dwelleth in you?"

John 3:16—a divine love. "God so loved the world, that he gave his only begotten Son, that whosoever believeth in him should not perish, but have everlasting life."

Preach the Word

All Scripture is given by inspiration of God.

God inspired the writing of the 66 inerrant books we call the Holy Bible, so He evidently wants people everywhere to hear what each of those books say. Pastors know both the joy and the stress of preparing sermons that accurately explain the text of Scripture and demonstrate the timeless applications of His Word to our lives today.

The Bible is a timeless book of divine origin, so it is vital for pastors of every age and in every culture to teach the entire counsel of God revealed through Scripture. And yet certain books of the Bible tend to be neglected. Some will preach almost exclusively from the New Testament and avoid the wonderful accounts of God's work in the Old Testament. Some will focus on the Pauline writings or on eschatology or on Psalms or other types of literature in the Bible.

But the fact remains that the Bible is one unified revelation of God, from Genesis to Revelation. No portion of Scripture should be neglected because it seems uncomfortable or even controversial. God wrote it for our benefit, and all of it is profitable.

Scripture:
2 Timothy 3:16

Eternity on Our Minds

*Set your affection on things above,
not on things on the earth.*

Scripture makes it clear that since the Fall, our earthly lives are temporal. The sin committed by Adam and Eve set death in motion, both physically and spiritually. How that must have grieved the Creator! And yet our Lord loved the first couple and their descendants so much that He provided a plan of redemption that would rescue His beloved creation from the ultimate consequences of that sin. Why?

Because eternity is on God's mind. Is it on ours?

Every new year brings with it a feeling of renewal, a sense of starting fresh with new plans, new commitments, and new opportunities. But how much of this newness is focused here on earth?

Paul's admonition to the Colossians reminds us that real living is not in the here and now, but in the glory to come, when the temporal becomes eternal. Why? Because that's where Christ is, and that's our promised destiny. Our citizenship is in heaven, not on this ball of dirt.

So we need to think with eternity on our minds; we need to plan with eternity on our minds. Doing so allows us a greater glimpse of the glory to come.

Scripture:

Colossians 3:1-4; John 3:16; Philippians 3:20

No Ordinary Day

When the centurion, and they that were with him, watching Jesus, saw the earthquake, and those things that were done, they feared greatly, saying, Truly this was the Son of God.

Christ's death and His resurrection three days later marked the most significant days in all of history. An innocent man died an ignominious death in place of you and me and every other sinner in the world. Of course, Jesus was no ordinary man. He was a perfect man, but also deity—the unique God-man. Only He could rescue mankind from spiritual and eternal damnation.

No wonder the death, burial, and resurrection of Christ were surrounded by unusual events witnessed by ordinary men and women in Jerusalem. The sun was obscured during the day. Tombs were opened, and saints were raised from the dead. The ground shook, and rocks were split open. The temple veil was torn from top to bottom. This was no ordinary day.

Jesus' death was no ordinary execution by the Romans. God let it be known that He was accomplishing a great work for all mankind.

Scripture:
Matthew 27:54; 1 John 2:2

Be Mine

God commendeth his love toward us, in that,
while we were yet sinners, Christ died for us.

As children, we received valentines from classmates. These messages somehow seemed to strike fear and trepidation in the boys each February. Most who celebrate love at this time are led only by giddy emotions rather than by love's more important characteristics.

As Christians, we are familiar with a deeper kind of love—agape love—that remains rock solid despite our feelings at any given moment. It's a mature love that was ultimately and perfectly expressed by God, who sacrificed His Son for us.

The simple fact is that God loved and chose us. And He loved us despite our sinfulness.

God chose the Jewish people from out of all the other peoples of the earth. Why? What was special about Abraham and his descendants? Were they a mighty people? A sophisticated people? A noble people? No. God earlier stated that it was because of His love that He chose to make Israel His own special possession.

And He's still saying that today. Not with cards and candy, but with daily demonstrations of His unwavering love.

Scripture:
Romans 5:8; Deuteronomy 14:2; 4:37; 10:15

God's Quickenings

Quicken thou me according to thy word.

The theme of Psalm 119 is the Word of God. Numerous times the psalmist asks God to quicken him; that is, to revive or give him life by means of His Word. "For the word of God is quick, and powerful, and sharper than any two-edged sword." Quickening produces several things:

Restoration. "My soul cleaveth unto the dust: quicken thou me according to thy word."

Comfort. "This is my comfort in my affliction: for thy word hath quickened me." Truly, it is the Word of God that brings comfort in all our afflictions.

Deliverance. "Plead my cause, and deliver me: quicken me according to thy word."

Guidance. "Turn away mine eyes from beholding vanity; and quicken thou me in thy way." Rather than turning aside into empty ways, we should allow God to guide us in the paths of righteousness.

Resolve. "I will never forget thy precepts: for with them thou hast quickened me." "Consider how I love thy precepts: quicken me, O LORD, according to thy lovingkindness."

Scripture:
Psalm 119:25,50,154,37,93,159

Love and Jealousy

Many waters cannot quench love,
neither can the floods drown it.

The undying love mentioned in our text is nothing less than intimate marital love. It is not a plaything. How many lives have been ruined because another did not abide within the proper parameters of love?

Our Lord taught, "They twain [two] shall be one flesh"—not three or four. From the beginning, a man and a woman were designed to be joined in holy matrimony. Proverbs pictures the emotion of a man enraged because another has committed adultery with his wife: "Jealousy is the rage of a man: therefore he will not spare in the day of vengeance."

The notion that marital love is a training ground for our relationship with the Lord is encouraged in Scripture. God complained that Israel was unfaithful to Him many times and lusted after other gods.

As our Creator and Savior, the Lord Jesus Christ deserves our faithfulness and undivided affection. His love for us is stronger even than death, for He experienced death on the cross so that we might experience the blessings of His love.

Scripture:
Song of Solomon 8:7; Matthew 19:5; Proverbs 6:32-35

Love's Redeeming Work

God, who is rich in mercy, for his great
love wherewith he loved us…

Redemption occurred because of God's great love for us. "God so loved the world, that he gave his only begotten Son." Redemption "is finished," Jesus cried. Verse three of the hymn "Christ the Lord Is Risen Today" celebrates this victory:

> Love's redeeming work is done, Allelujah!
> Fought the fight, the battle won, Allelujah!
> Death in vain forbids Him rise, Allelujah!
> Christ hath opened paradise, Allelujah!

As Charles Wesley wrote this, he had more in mind than Christ's resurrection. "I am he that liveth, and was dead; and, behold, I am alive for evermore." And then He promised, "To him that overcometh will I give to eat of the tree of life, which is in the midst of the paradise of God."

How can we gain sweet redemption and enter into this paradise? "If thou shalt confess with thy mouth the Lord Jesus, and shalt believe in thine heart that God hath raised him from the dead, thou shalt be saved."

Scripture:
Ephesians 2:4-6; John 3:16; 19:30; Revelation 1:18; 2:7;
Romans 10:9

God Is Love

He that loveth not knoweth
not God; for God is love.

"God is love." Everyone responds to love, and everything seems empty without it. Little wonder then that the Scripture also says, "He that loveth not knoweth not God." If God were truly known, love would be the result, not hate.

God's love is not merely a theoretical concept or a theological doctrine. "Herein is love, not that we loved God, but that he loved us, and sent his Son to be the propitiation for our sins."

We are given a glimpse of God looking for Adam and Eve after their disobedience. One godly preacher noted, "When you read God's first question to man, 'Where art thou?' as though He were some sort of policeman seeking a fugitive from justice, you do not know anything about God. You must read it as though God were a brokenhearted father looking for a lost child."

God aches to help us. He loves us more than we can understand or feel. "The LORD God, merciful and gracious, long-suffering, and abundant in goodness and truth"—He *loves* us.

Scripture:

1 John 4:8,10; Genesis 3:9; Exodus 34:6

We Have the Mind of Christ

God hath not given us the spirit of fear; but
of power, and of love, and of a sound mind.

Paul encourages the believers in Rome, "Be ye transformed by the renewing of your mind." He told the Corinthians, "We have the mind of Christ."

The Lord Jesus commanded, "Love the Lord thy God... with all thy mind." He also said we must have implicit faith in the Word of God: "Neither be ye of doubtful mind...O fools, and slow of heart to believe all that the prophets have spoken." One should also "put on...humbleness of mind" and seek to discipline his mind. As Peter says, "Gird up the loins of your mind, be sober." Along with this, we should develop mature thinking—"in understanding be men."

We should not allow our minds to dwell on the vain imaginations of those "professing themselves to be wise" in the "wisdom of this world," which will soon "come to naught." It is us, not they, to whom God has given a "sound mind."

Scripture:
2 Timothy 1:7; 2 Corinthians 4:4; Romans 12:2; 1:21-22;
1 Corinthians 2:16; 14:20; Matthew 22:37; Luke 12:29; 24:25;
Colossians 3:12; 1 Peter 1:13

Love Not the World

*Love not the world, neither the
things that are in the world.*

The Greek word translated "world" in this verse is *cosmos*, referring to the world as an organized system. Paul warned against walking "according to the course of this world." Satan is the one who set its course, for "the whole world lieth in wickedness."

The world does not love us! "If the world hate you, ye know that it hated me before it hated you." Yet how diligently we work to acquire possessions and attain high positions in the world system. "The lust of the flesh, and the lust of the eyes, and the pride of life, is not of the Father, but is of the world." Instead, we should "overcome the world."

But we *should* love the world in one important way: "God so loved the world, that he gave his only begotten Son." Christ prayed, "As thou hast sent me into the world, even so have I also sent them into the world." He did not love the world's possessions or pleasures or positions, but its *people*! Like Jesus, we too must love them and show them the way back to their Creator and Savior.

Scripture:

1 John 2:15-16; John 5:18; 15:18; 3:16; 17:18; Ephesians 2:2

Love Thy Neighbor

Who is my neighbor?

Jesus affirmed that the greatest commandments were to love God and to love "thy neighbor as thyself." A lawyer responded by asking, "Who is my neighbor?" Jesus answered by telling the story of the good Samaritan and concluded by saying, "Go, and do thou likewise."

A neighbor is not necessarily someone whose home is near ours or even one who is an acquaintance. The Samaritan had never met the robbed and wounded traveler. He wasn't even a fellow countryman.

However, he was a neighbor because (1) their paths crossed, (2) the victim had a real need, and (3) the Samaritan could meet that need. Since all three criteria were satisfied, the Samaritan had an obligation, and the Lord has told us to do likewise.

In loving one's neighbor in the same way we love ourselves, we do what we would want to have done for us if the roles were reversed. However, there is something more. The love of which the Lord spoke here is *agape*, or unselfish love. In the highest sense, love for one's neighbor means seeking God's will in and for the one who is loved.

Scripture:
Luke 10:27,29,37

Fervent Love

*Seeing ye have purified your souls in obeying
the truth through the Spirit unto unfeigned
love of the brethren, see that ye love one
another with a pure heart fervently.*

This passage uses two different words for two different kinds of love.

The first implies the brotherly love that results from obedience to the teachings of Scripture, through the work of the Holy Spirit, and the accompanying purification of our souls. Yet it has no standards of right and wrong and no provision for self-sacrifice for the other's benefit. Therefore, it can degenerate into a self-centered relationship.

The second is *agape* love, or God's self-sacrificial love. "God so loved the world that he gave his only begotten Son." It is part of the "fruit of the Spirit" and is described in detail in 1 Corinthians 13. "God is love."

"Fervent" love is literally that which is "stretched out, extended to the limit." It must come from "a pure heart." The well-being of others is the sole motivation for this kind of love, and this motivation is sorely needed to adequately demonstrate God's love.

Scripture:
1 Peter 1:22; John 3:16; Galatians 5:22; 1 John 4:8

How to Love

*Seeing ye have purified your souls in obeying
the truth through the Spirit unto unfeigned
love of the brethren, see that ye love one
another with a pure heart fervently.*

We are to love all people, even our enemies in one sense, but here Peter speaks specifically of "love of the brethren."

This is not merely brotherly love, but *agape*, sacrificial love, like Christ's. "He laid down his life for us: and we ought to lay down our lives for the brethren."

It should also be unfeigned love. "Let love be without dissimulation," or hypocrisy. It is also pure love—spiritual, not physical. Finally, it should be fervent, or strong and enduring.

So our love for other Christians should be sacrificial, sincere, chaste, and enduring. And all of this is predicated on obedience to God's Word as we are "obeying the truth through the Spirit."

"We know that we have passed from death unto life, because we love the brethren," John says. "He that loveth not his brother abideth in death." Therefore, we must see that we love one another fervently and with a pure heart.

Scripture:
1 Peter 1:22; Matthew 5:44; 1 John 3:14,16; Romans 12:9

Courage and Strength

*Wait on the LORD: be of good courage, and he shall
strengthen thine heart: wait, I say, on the LORD.*

A strong heart that waits on the Lord is of good courage.
Waiting on the Lord is the joyful expectation of the just
resolution of all things. "Be of good courage" can also be translated, "become mighty."

We become courageous because we base our motives
and actions on God's Word, we act courageously on behalf
of those we love, and we commit the results to God as He
strengthens our hearts. We become courageous because we
obey God's Word, and it takes courage to obey God's Word.
"Only be thou strong and very courageous," God told Joshua,
"that thou mayest observe to do according to all the law." The
Hebrew word for this courage is also used to describe the
strong heart in today's verse.

When God strengthens our hearts, He establishes within
us a determination that He is indeed worthy of our trust and
devotion. He says to us, "Fear thou not; for I am with thee: be
not dismayed; for I am thy God: I will strengthen thee."

Scripture:

Psalm 27:14; Joshua 1:7; Isaiah 41:10

God's Love for All the World

*The Lord is not slack concerning his promise...
not willing that any should perish, but
that all should come to repentance.*

Genesis 3:15, the Bible's first promise of a Redeemer, indicates that God intended salvation for all mankind, not just Adam and Eve. And in the Noahic covenant, God made an "everlasting covenant between God and every living creature of all flesh that is upon the earth."

As we see His plan unfold, we may be tempted to doubt that God wanted all humans to experience His salvation, for in Genesis 12 God focuses on one man—Abram. From Abram, Israel became the people of God and experienced His special guidance and blessing.

But in Genesis 12:2, God not only says to Abram, "I will make of thee a great nation, and I will bless thee," but also promises that "in thee shall all families of the earth be blessed." God shared His great love for all by declaring Israel to be a whole race of priests on behalf of the rest of the nations.

Eventually, the ultimate love of God was realized when "God sent forth his Son, made of a woman," "that the world through him might be saved."

Scripture:
2 Peter 3:9; Genesis 9:16; 12:2-3; Isaiah 42:6;
Galatians 4:4; John 3:17

Love Is Obedience

This is the love of God, that we keep his commandments: and his commandments are not grievous.

John was the disciple who had a special love for Jesus and "whom Jesus loved." He wrote that this type of love is not an emotional or sentimental feeling, but total obedience to Him: "If ye love me, keep my commandments." "But whoso keepeth his word, in him verily is the love of God perfected; hereby know we that we are in him." "And this is love, that we walk after his commandments." Obeying His commandment, which He gave because He loves us, proves our love for Him.

The other side is love toward others. "This commandment have we from him, that he who loveth God love his brother also." John also wrote "that we love one another" and "these things I command you, that ye love one another." Paul added, "Thou shalt love thy neighbor as thyself. Love worketh no ill to his neighbor: therefore love is the fulfilling of the law."

Loving others works no ill, but seeks their greater good.

Scripture:
1 John 5:3; 2:5; 4:21; John 15:17; 14:15; 2 John 5-6;
Romans 13:9-10

Life, Light, and Love

All things were made by him; and without
him was not any thing made that was made.
In him was life; and the life was the light
of men. And the light shineth in darkness;
and the darkness comprehended it not.

John wrote about God as life (*zoe*), light (*phos*), and love (*agape*) more than any other New Testament writer.

Christ has existed "from the beginning" and is the Creator of physical life on earth. He is also "the life," and "in him was life," denoting salvation and eternal life based on His own atonement for sin.

And not only did Christ create physical light and light sources, but He *is* light, or the revelation of the things of God to people. His "life was the light of men."

But most of all, "God is love." John wrote, "God so loved the world," and His undeserved love drove Him to give "his only begotten Son, that whosoever believeth in him should not perish, but have everlasting life." "Herein is love...that he loved us, and sent his Son...for our sins."

Scripture:
John 1:3-5; 20:2; 14:6; 3:16; 1 John 4:8; 1:5; 1:1; 4:10;
Colossians 1:16; Acts 17:28; Genesis 1:3,14

The Measure of Better

*Better is little with the fear of the LORD than
great treasure and trouble therewith. Better
is a dinner of herbs where love is, than
a stalled ox and hatred therewith.*

The true measure of "worth" has nothing to do with money. In fact, Proverbs is filled with cases where more money results in less happiness and contentment.

"Better is a little with righteousness than great revenues without right." "Better is a dry morsel, and quietness therewith, than an house full of sacrifices with strife." "Better it is to be of an humble spirit with the lowly, than to divide the spoil with the proud." "Better is the poor that walketh in his uprightness, than he that is perverse in his ways, though he be rich."

This is a lesson that the many affluent Christian men and women of our prosperous nation urgently need to learn today. In the New Testament, Paul wrote to his young disciple Timothy that "godliness with contentment is great gain." "But they that will be rich fall into temptation and a snare, and into many foolish and hurtful lusts…and pierced themselves through with many sorrows."

Scripture:

Proverbs 15:16-17; 16:8,19; 17:1; 28:6; 1 Timothy 6:6,9-10

Even as Christ

*Husbands, love your wives, even as Christ also
loved the church, and gave himself for it.*

In recent years, many have either misapplied or ignored what the Bible says regarding family roles. Perhaps the clearest passage on this subject is Ephesians 5:21-33. In "submitting yourselves one to another in the fear of God," the primary role of the wife is to submit to her husband's headship, and the husband's role is to self-sacrifically love his wife.

These roles were given when mankind was cursed, so they run contrary to our natures, though they are not impossible to achieve.

As we look at the example of Christ and His church, the wife submits to her husband's headship, "for the husband is the head of the wife, even as Christ is the head of the church: and he is the savior of the body. Therefore as the church is subject unto Christ, so let the wives be to their own husbands in every thing."

Likewise, Christ gave Himself for the church that He might "sanctify and cleanse it." Therefore, husbands are to love their wives as Christ loved us, for "while we were yet sinners, Christ died for us."

Scripture:
Ephesians 5:25; Genesis 3:16; Romans 5:8

Charity or Love?

Though I speak with the tongues of men and
of angels, and have not charity, I am become
as sounding brass, or a tinkling cymbal.

The word *agape* is translated "love" in most modern Bible translations. In the King James Version, it is translated "love" more often than it is rendered "charity." The translators knew the word did not mean giving to the poor, for they translated the third verse, "Though I bestow all my goods to feed the poor…and have not charity, it profiteth me nothing."

And they evidently knew that *agape* did not mean "charity" in today's sense. But neither does *agape* refer to the most common modern concepts of "love"—romantic, erotic, or brotherly love.

Actually, the original English concept of charity—a genuine and unselfish concern for others—is also the true biblical meaning of *agape*. In fact, no single English word today really seems to fit, perhaps because we have almost lost the very virtue that the word "charity" once expressed. But regardless of how we say it, our lives desperately need to show *agape*, for God Himself is *agape*.

Scripture:
1 Corinthians 13:1,3; 1 John 4:8

The Instruction of Thy Father

*My son, hear the instruction of thy father,
and forsake not the law of thy mother.*

The Proverbs for Solomon—perhaps compiled by his father, David—are laid out in the form of 14 lessons that each begin with "my son" or its equivalent, "O ye children."

The first of these lessons urges children to heed the counsel of their parents. Paul also emphasizes this in the New Testament: "Children, obey your parents in the Lord: for this is right. Honor thy father and thy mother; which is the first commandment with promise."

Each of the 14 lessons stresses the importance of young people heeding God's Word. Wise counsel, learning, discretion, instruction, knowledge, understanding, and wisdom are promised to those who know, love, and obey God's Word.

"My son, if thou wilt receive my words, and hide my commandments with thee; so that thou incline thine ear unto wisdom, and apply thine heart to understanding; yea, if thou criest after knowledge, and liftest up thy voice for understanding; if thou seekest her as silver, and searchest for her as for hid treasures; then shalt thou understand the fear of the LORD, and find the knowledge of God."

Scripture:
Proverbs 1:8,2; 2:1-5; 3:1,11,21; 4:1,10,20; 5:1,7; 6:20; 7:1,24; 8:32;
Ephesians 6:1-2

Love and the Heart

Jesus said unto him, Thou shalt love the
Lord thy God with all thy heart, and with
all thy soul, and with all thy mind.

According to Jesus, this is "the great commandment of the law," and this is also the first verse in the New Testament to associate love (*agape*) and the heart (*kardia*).

Kardia, from which comes the English word "cardiology," is used often in the Bible but almost never refers to the physical organ. The *kardia* is almost always the emotional and spiritual components of human nature—"the hidden man of the heart." *Agape* can only be expressed out of a heart that has been made pure. Peter wrote to believers, "See that ye love one another with a pure heart fervently." Paul wrote to young Timothy, "The end of the commandment is charity [*agape*] out of a pure heart, and of a good conscience, and of faith unfeigned."

Jesus reminds us of our first priority and the source of our love for others: "Love the Lord thy God with all thy heart, and with all thy soul, and with all thy mind, and with all thy strength: this is the first commandment."

Scripture:

Matthew 22:37; 1 Peter 1:22; 1 Timothy 1:5; Mark 12:30

The Greatest Love

*Take now thy son, thine only son Isaac, whom thou
lovest…and offer him there for a burnt offering.*

There are many types of love in the world. But what is the
greatest love?

We encounter love in Genesis, particularly in Abraham's
relationship with his son Isaac. But the very God who promised this father his son tells him to sacrifice him!

From the New Testament, we know that this entire scene
is a remarkable type of the heavenly Father and His willingness to offer His own beloved Son, Jesus, in sacrifice for the
sin of the world. The love of this human father for his human
son is an earthly picture of the great eternal love of the heavenly Father for His only begotten Son.

God the Father's love for God the Son is the ultimate
source of all love, for it existed before the world began. When
Jesus prayed to His Father the night before His death, He confirmed this great truth: "For thou lovedst me before the foundation of the world."

Indeed, "God is love," and this eternal love is the foundation of all true human love here on earth.

Scripture:
Genesis 22:2; Hebrews 11:17-18; John 17:24; 1 John 4:8

No More Fears

What time I am afraid, I will trust in thee.

In the Bible's first mention of fear, Adam said to God, "I heard thy voice in the garden, and I was afraid."

Indeed, those who ignore or reject God's Word should be afraid, for "it is a fearful thing to fall into the hands of the living God." The Bible's final reference to fear gives the same warning to sinners of all the ages: "The fearful, and unbelieving…shall have their part in the lake which burneth with fire and brimstone: which is the second death."

However, the Old Testament psalmist wrote, "I sought the LORD, and he heard me, and delivered me from all my fears." God has already endured everything we could ever fear, even death itself, that through His victory He might "deliver them who through fear of death were all their lifetime subject to bondage." Therefore, since "the LORD is my light and my salvation; whom shall I fear? the LORD is the strength of my life; of whom shall I be afraid?"

Scripture:

Psalm 56:3; 34:4; 27:1; Genesis 3:10;
Hebrews 10:31; 2:15; Revelation 21:8

Whom Having Not Seen,
Ye Love

…whom having not seen, ye love; in whom,
though now ye see him not, yet believing, ye
rejoice with joy unspeakable and full of glory.

Many of the earliest believers followed Christ because they heard the gospel from His own lips and saw Him raise the dead and heal the sick and blind. They believed because they had seen. Christ, however, reserved a special place for those who believed but had never seen.

In John 20:24-29, Christ appeared to His disciples after the resurrection, but Thomas was not present. When the disciples told Thomas that they had seen the Lord, he said he had to see for himself the wounds in His side, His hands, and His feet. The next time Christ appeared to His disciples, Thomas was there, and Christ invited him to see His wounds. In response, Thomas declared, "My Lord and my God." And Christ replied, "Thomas, because thou hast seen me, thou hast believed: blessed are they that have not seen, and yet have believed."

So we rejoice with joy unspeakable and full of glory, "receiving the end of [our] faith, even the salvation of [our] souls."

Scripture:
1 Peter 1:8-9; John 20:24-29

Finding Grace

Noah found grace in the eyes of the Lord.

In the midst of a violent and wicked society, Noah was "a just man and perfect in his generations," so he "found grace in the eyes of the Lord."

God's grace is not earned or learned, but it is found! "The eyes of the Lord run to and fro throughout the whole earth, to show himself strong in the behalf of them whose heart is perfect toward him." The Lord had to search diligently to find a man whose heart was open toward Him. But when He found Noah, "Noah found grace"!

The angel Gabriel said to Mary, "Fear not, Mary: for thou hast found favor [literally, 'grace'] with God." Thus, Noah was chosen to save a believing remnant from destruction in the Flood, and Mary was chosen to give birth to the One who would take away the world's sin.

It is the same today. Although "the grace of God that bringeth salvation hath appeared to all men," only "few there be that find it." God's grace is available, but it takes a seeing heart and a hearing soul to find it.

Scripture:
Genesis 6:8-9,13; 2 Chronicles 16:9; Luke 1:30;
Titus 2:11; Matthew 7:14

Mine Eyes Have Seen

*Mine eyes have seen thy salvation, which
thou hast prepared before the face of all
people; a light to lighten the Gentiles,
and the glory of thy people Israel.*

The prophet Simeon said this as he held the infant Jesus. With his physical eyes, he saw a baby, but with eyes of faith, he saw much more.

He could see the very Son of God on a cross dying for the sins of all. Almost 2000 years earlier, Jacob had cried out, "I have waited for thy salvation, O LORD." And now Simeon had seen Him!

Among the Jews, who rejected Gentiles as "aliens from the commonwealth of Israel," Simeon could also see the fulfillment of the all-but-forgotten messianic prophecy: "I the LORD have called thee in righteousness, and...will...give thee for a covenant of the people, for a light of the Gentiles."

And though Christ was "set for the fall and rising again of many in Israel; and for a sign which shall be spoken against," He shall eventually "reign over the house of Jacob for ever; and of his kingdom there shall be no end."

Scripture:
Luke 2:30-32,34; 1:33; Genesis 49:18; Isaiah 42:6;
Ephesians 2:12-13

Living in Christ

For to me to live is Christ, and to die is gain.

Our daily activities can be transformed in the Lord Jesus Christ's presence. Like the two disciples on the road to Emmaus, when "Jesus himself drew near, and went with them," we can testify, "Did not our heart burn within us, while he talked with us by the way?"

Or, like Andrew and another disciple (probably John) who "abode with him that day" and then desired to bring others to Him, our love for the Lord and concern for others can grow with Him.

Mary of Bethany "sat at Jesus' feet, and heard his word," and we too can hear Him by the Holy Spirit.

We can even say with Paul, "I am crucified with Christ," but nevertheless we are "alive unto God through Jesus Christ," if indeed we resolve by His enabling "that henceforth we should not serve sin."

Finally, like all those of every generation who "love his appearing," we can "look for him," knowing that one day we shall "ever be with the Lord."

Scripture:

Philippians 1:21; Luke 24:15,32; 10:39; John 1:39-42;
Galatians 2:20; Romans 6:11,6; 2 Timothy 4:8;
Hebrews 9:28; 1 Thessalonians 4:17

The Extended Family

He shall receive an hundredfold now in this time,
houses, and brethren, and sisters, and mothers,
and children, and lands, with persecutions;
and in the world to come eternal life.

As Mary's eldest Son, Jesus was responsible for his mother's well-being. As He died, He made sure another "son" could take care of her—John, who in turn cared for Mary as he would for his own mother. Of the one who does the will of the heavenly Father, Jesus said, "The same is my brother, and sister, and mother."

John seems indeed to have grasped the broader message when he addressed believers as "my little children." Paul, similarly, called Timothy "my own son in the faith." He wrote that Timothy should treat an elder "as a father; and the younger men as brethren; the elder women as mothers; the younger as sisters." In Mark 10, we learn that broken physical relationships that occur because of faith in Christ will be replaced "an hundredfold…brethren, sisters, fathers, mothers, wives, children."

Because of Jesus, believers have been brought into a big family of faith.

Scripture:
Mark 10:30; Luke 7:13; John 19:26-27; Matthew 12:50; 19:29;
1 John 2:1; 1 Timothy 1:2; 5:1-2

Accepted in the Beloved

…to the praise of the glory of his grace, wherein
he hath made us accepted in the beloved.

Those saved by God's grace through Christ have been "accepted" by the Lord. The Greek word occurs one other time in the New Testament, when the angel Gabriel said to Mary, "Hail, thou that art highly favored, the Lord is with thee: blessed art thou among women." We are not merely accepted; we are highly favored by God!

Although Christ is called God's "beloved Son" seven times in the New Testament, only one other time is He referred to as the beloved: "Behold my servant, whom I have chosen; my beloved, in whom my soul is well pleased: I will put my spirit upon him."

God's love for His Son is the source of every other love in the universe: "Father…thou lovedst me before the foundation of the world." This is what it means to be highly favored in the beloved!

We who are in Him are predestined to be with Him in glory, to behold His glory, and forever, as redeemed sinners saved by grace through faith, to be "to the praise of the glory of his grace."

Scripture:

Ephesians 1:6; Luke 1:28; John 17:24; Matthew 12:18

Working No Ill to the Preborn

Love worketh no ill to his neighbor:
therefore love is the fulfilling of the law.

Some say that the New Testament is silent on the subject of abortion, but Paul, after reminding his readers of the laws against various sins and the obligation to love our neighbors, added, "Love worketh no ill to his neighbor." It is unlikely that the apostle, who was set apart from his mother's womb, would have excluded the most fragile among us in his concept of neighbors.

When Luke, a physician, recorded Pharaoh's order to kill "young children," he used the same word for "children" as he did to describe the preborn John the Baptist: "When Elisabeth heard the salutation of Mary, the babe leaped in her womb." If Pharaoh's killing of babies was wrong, how can any Christian believe that Scripture allows the killing of even younger babies by abortion?

Children need protection, and they are dependent on our love. Paul wrote that "love is the fulfilling of the law." Let us obey this law, reiterated in the New Testament, and love every single child, because "love worketh no ill to his neighbor."

Scripture:

Romans 13:9-10; Galatians 1:15; Acts 7:19; Luke 1:41

What Jesus Saw

The two disciples heard him speak…Jesus
turned, and saw them following.

John wrote seven times about Jesus seeing something that led Him to action. The two disciples mentioned in our text followed Him, and their lives were changed forever. Then "Jesus saw Nathanael," who became one of the twelve disciples.

A crippled man lay near the pool of Bethesda in Jerusalem. But "when Jesus saw him," He healed him. In Galilee, "Jesus… saw a great company come unto him," and He fed them all with just five loaves and two small fish. Also, "Jesus…saw a man which was blind from his birth" and opened his eyes. In Bethany, Lazarus was dead for four days. When He finally came, "Jesus therefore saw…[Mary] weeping," and He also wept and then resurrected Lazarus!

Then, as He was dying on the cross, His mother and His beloved disciple John were there. "When Jesus therefore saw his mother," He commissioned John to care for her in His place.

Our Lord Jesus sees our needs and cares. And one day soon, He "shall wipe away all tears from [our] eyes."

Scripture:
John 1:37-38; 5:6; 6:5; 9:1; 11:33; 19:26; Revelation 21:4

Christ's Active Obedience

*When Jesus therefore saw his mother, and the
disciple standing by, whom he loved, he saith
unto his mother, Woman, behold thy son! Then
saith he to the disciple, Behold thy mother!*

When Adam and Eve were tested in the garden by our
Lord, they proved themselves disobedient.

Jesus came to bear the weight of and punishment for
Adam's sin, revealing His passive obedience to the law. But
He also established His perfect righteousness. This was His
active obedience to the law.

We see both aspects of this great salvation in John 19. As
the Lord of glory hung on a cross, He was made sin for His
people, and He passively received the judgment due them. But
He also was actively pursuing righteousness. The law required
that sons honor their mothers, and He honored His mother
not only by bearing her sins (to her eternal benefit) but also by
appointing John to care for her earthly needs.

All His life, the Lord actively kept the law for His people. As the sin of the first man was imputed to all in Adam, so
the perfect righteousness of the Lord Jesus is imputed to all in
Him—including Mary, His mother.

Scripture:

John 19:26-27; Exodus 20:12; Deuteronomy 5:16

The Degrees of Faith

I will hide my face from them…for they are a very
froward generation, children in whom is no faith.

Some have no faith in the true God at all, like the apostate Israelites mentioned in today's verse. There are many in our present "froward generation" ("froward" means "perverse") as well who have forgotten their Creator.

But some are like the sinful woman who came to Jesus in tearful repentance and received a saving faith. Jesus blessed her: "Thy faith hath saved thee; go in peace." To the disciples, who had little spiritual discernment or maturity, Christ's rebuke was, "O ye of little faith!"

But James described those whom God chose, who are "the poor of this world [but] rich in faith." Abraham "was strong in faith, giving glory to God; and being fully persuaded that, what he had promised, he was able also to perform." Similarly, Stephen was "a man full of faith and of the Holy Ghost."

Tragically, some have no faith, and God eternally hides His face from them. But how wonderful it will be to have strong and full faith when we meet the Lord!

Scripture:
Deuteronomy 32:20; Luke 7:37,50; Matthew 16:8;
Romans 4:20-21; James 2:5; Acts 6:5

God's "Very Good" Creation

*God saw every thing that he had made,
and, behold, it was very good.*

God's creation of the "very good" universe occupies just two chapters of the Bible before Satan and sin enter, but the Hebrew word *towb* ("good") is used throughout the Old Testament. For instance, *towb* described the "fair" and "beautiful" Esther, the "best" men, and the "better" of a host of comparisons. "Bountiful," "fine," "joyful," "pleasant," "precious," "prosperity," and "sweet" are just a few of the many other translations of *towb* that God used to describe His creation.

Six times throughout the creation week, God saw that His creation was "good." But at the end of the sixth day, He pronounced it "very good." It makes little sense to believe that God could have made such a statement at the end of some evolutionary struggle that left multitudes of fossil remains in petrified testimony to their final battle with death.

"For whatsoever things were written aforetime were written for our learning, that we through patience and comfort of the Scriptures might have hope." The doctrine of a "very good" creation by an almighty Creator will stand for eternity.

Scripture:
Genesis 1:4,10,12,18,21,25,31; Esther 1:11; 2:7;
2 Kings 10:3; Romans 15:4

No Adultery

Thou shalt not commit adultery.

God created one man and one woman for that man to marry.

Adam recognized the sanctity of marriage, and Christ verified and reaffirmed this fidelity. Adultery "murders" a marriage and was punished with the death penalty. The Bible also gives several parallel restrictions. Premarital sex and prostitution are forbidden. The perversion of homosexuality and the practice of religious sexual rites are also banned. God abhorred such behavior because these sins defiled the land. Perhaps even more damning than the physical sins was the false worship of other gods.

The Lord Jesus equated lust and adultery, noting that the heart is the source of all evil actions. In fact, in the New Testament, any worldly association is whoredom, and such friendship is enmity with God. Unfortunately, we are surrounded by an overt promotion of such behavior, enticing all to engage freely. It is distributed to us through books, movies, TV, Internet, music, fashion, and associations. The Christian must conform to biblical standards and not to the world's tolerance or permission.

Scripture:

Genesis 2:18,23-25; Exodus 20:14; Deuteronomy 23:17-18; Matthew 5:27-28; 1 Corinthians 6:13-18; James 4:4; 1 John 2:15-17

The Creator of Marriage

*Have ye not read, that he which made them at
the beginning made them male and female?*

God created Adam and Eve as full-grown adults in the beginning, united as husband and wife—not a population of primates slowly evolving into people over millions of years. Skeptical scientists and liberal theologians who have insisted that the creation account in Genesis 1 and 2 contradicts itself stand rebuked by the Creator Himself, for Christ quoted from both Genesis 1:27 and 2:24, accepting both of them as valid, historical, and complementary accounts of the same event. Furthermore, He confirmed the Genesis teachings that the first and most basic of all human institutions is the home and that the Creator designed marriage to be monogamous and permanent.

Although modern evangelicals have differing opinions on divorce and remarriage, these variations were not present in the beginning. Paul even used the ideal marriage to describe the permanent union of Christ and His church. God, in His grace, forgives confessed and forsaken sin—even sin against the marriage covenant—but this does not eliminate the accompanying suffering and heartbreak.

How much better it is to follow God's creative purpose in all things, especially at home.

Scripture:
Matthew 19:4-6; Ephesians 5:25-27

Relative Hatred

*If any man come to me, and hate not his
father, and mother, and wife, and children,
and brethren, and sisters, yea, and his
own life also, he cannot be my disciple.*

Jesus is not urging hatred of one's relatives here. Rather, He is referring to hatred relative to one's love for God and His will.

Jesus commanded us to love our neighbors and even our enemies, so surely He expected us to love our families. But love for God must be paramount. "Thou shalt love the Lord thy God with all thy heart, and with all thy soul, and with all thy strength, and with all thy mind."

Sometimes, "a man's foes shall be they of his own household" if he loves God. If faced with the choice, the one who would truly be Christ's disciple must follow Him.

Still, we are commanded, "honor thy father and mother" and "provoke not your children to anger." Even Jesus' mission was initially rejected by His family, but He remained patient, all the while placing God first.

Scripture:
Luke 14:26; 10:27; Matthew 5:44; 10:36; Ephesians 6:2;
Colossians 3:21; John 7:5

All Rights Reserved

*Blessed be thy advice, and blessed be thou, which
hast kept me this day from coming to shed blood,
and from avenging myself with mine own hand.*

Abigail's husband, Nabal, selfishly slighted David and his
men. Abigail prevented David from punishing Nabal,
but David was eventually avenged, for "it came to pass about
ten days after, that the LORD smote Nabal."

Paul wrote, "Avenge not yourselves…for it is written, vengeance is mine; I will repay, saith the Lord."

Nabal's shepherds had been guarded by David's men, but
when the time came to be recognized as protectors, David and
his men were rebuffed by Nabal and sent away. This is a picture of Christ, our deliverer and protector, being rejected, and
then God, in righteousness, judging the rejecter.

"God so loved the world, that he gave his only begotten
Son, that whosoever believeth in him should not perish, but
have everlasting life," but "he that believeth not the Son shall
not see life; but the wrath of God abideth on him." God has
reserved all rights to vengeance on those who reject the salvation that He, in His own great love, reserved the right to purchase.

Scripture:

1 Samuel 25:33,38; Romans 12:19; 2 Timothy 4:8; John 3:16,36

Allegories in Scripture

*Which things are an allegory: for these are the
two covenants; the one from the mount Sinai,
which gendereth to bondage, which is Agar.*

Paul wrote that the conflict between Hagar and Sarah (the mothers of Ishmael and Isaac, respectively) was a spiritual allegory, depicting the conflict between law and grace.

Early church fathers indulged in such an allegorical approach to Scripture, attempting to harmonize Christianity with Greek philosophy. Modern theological liberals often do the same thing, particularly with the Genesis account of creation. The allegorical interpretation of creation denies its historicity but tries to retain its supposed spiritual message by finding a devotional application in its narratives.

However, the only narrative actually called an allegory in Scripture is the one Paul refers to in Galatians. In fact, this is the only time the Greek word *allegoreo* ("allegory") is used in the Bible at all. Paul's use of the word does not suggest Hagar and Sarah were not real. Numerous other New Testament references to Abraham and to Sarah all clearly treat them as real persons.

This biblical example shows that if we draw allegorical applications from its historical records, it can only be on the basis that the events were real.

Scripture:

Galatians 4:24

How to Save Your Life

Remember Lot's wife.

Scripture records nothing Lot's wife said or did, with one exception, and yet Jesus wants us to remember her. When God tried to save Lot and his family from the destruction of Sodom and Gomorrah, "his wife looked back from behind him, and she became a pillar of salt."

This strange miracle really happened, and the Lord Jesus confirmed it as He did the destruction of Sodom. The reason to remember her? "Whosoever shall seek to save his life shall lose it; and whosoever shall lose his life shall preserve it."

Therefore, we should "remember Lot's wife" whenever we are tempted to hang on to a comfortable lifestyle in a wicked world. Lot himself was rather worldly minded, but when he consented to flee, his wife lagged "behind him" and "looked back," perhaps grieving over the imminent loss of her material comforts and social position. The Lord's long-suffering patience finally ended, and her carnal desire to save her old life caused her to lose her whole life.

"For what is a man profited, if he shall gain the whole world, and lose his own soul?"

Scripture:
Luke 17:32-33,28-29; Genesis 19:26; Matthew 16:26

A Time to Die

*To every thing there is a season, and a time
to every purpose under the heaven.*

God "worketh all things after the counsel of his own will,"
and even when we may not understand how a particular
event can be purposeful or beautiful, we can have faith that if
it occurs in God's time for it, it is.

The time of our birth is not under our control, but we can
certainly have a part in determining the occurrence of all the
other 13 "times" mentioned in Ecclesiastes—even the time of
death. Unless we are living at the time of Christ's return, each
of us will die. God has appointed that time, and it is wrong to
shorten that by suicide or careless living.

David said, "My times are in thy hand," and like him, we
should seek to please God as long as He allows us to live. And
when our time is finished, we pray He will enable us to die in
a manner that pleases Him as well.

None of us knows that ordained "time to die," so we must
seek daily to "walk in wisdom…redeeming the time."

Scripture:

Ecclesiastes 3:1-2,11; Romans 8:28; Psalm 31:15; Colossians 4:5

Living Waters

My spouse…[is] a spring shut up, a
fountain sealed…a well of living waters.

The first verse referring to "living water" appears in the Song of Solomon and describes the character of a bride as seen by her bridegroom, symbolic of the Lord and His people.

But in Jeremiah, God laments, "My people…have forsaken me the fountain of living waters." "They have forsaken the LORD, the fountain of living waters."

But one day they shall return, and "living waters shall go out from Jerusalem."

In the New Testament, the Lord Jesus used this metaphor for Himself: "If thou knewest the gift of God…he would have given thee living water." "The water that I shall give him shall be in him a well of water springing up into everlasting life."

Later, He cried out, "If any man thirst, let him come unto me, and drink. He that believeth on me …out of his belly shall flow rivers of living water."

And for those who die for the Lord's sake, "[He] shall lead them unto living fountains of waters: and God shall wipe away all tears from their eyes."

Scripture:
Song of Solomon 4:12-15; Jeremiah 2:13; 17:13; Zechariah 14:8-9; John 4:10,14; 7:37-38; Revelation 7:17

The New Jerusalem

Behold, I create Jerusalem a
rejoicing, and her people a joy.

Jerusalem has been a city of conflict and sorrow, and her people have long suffered under oppressors not only in Jerusalem (ironically, "city of peace") but all throughout the world.

The ultimate fulfillment of this striking prophecy can only be when we (like John in his vision) see "the holy city, new Jerusalem, coming down from God out of heaven, prepared as a bride adorned for her husband." In that day, "God shall wipe away all tears from their eyes; and there shall be no more death, neither sorrow, nor crying, neither shall there be any more pain: for the former things are passed away."

Since the new Jerusalem will come down from heaven, it must now be in heaven, where Christ has gone to prepare a place for us. Our Creator-Redeemer has created this new Jerusalem as our eternal dwelling place, as well as the new heavens and new earth.

Isaiah ends his remarkable prophecy with this wonderful assurance: "As the new heavens and the new earth, which I will make, shall remain before me, saith the LORD, so shall your seed and your name remain."

Scripture:
Isaiah 65:18; 66:22; Revelation 21:2-4; John 14:2

Garments of Salvation

I will greatly rejoice in the LORD...for he hath
clothed me with the garments of salvation, he
hath covered me with the robe of righteousness.

One of the beautiful biblical metaphors of salvation is that of clothing appropriate for coming into God's presence. We cannot make or purchase it; it must be prepared and provided by God.

Adam and Eve tried wearing fig leaves, but that didn't work. So God first had to slay two innocent animals, and then He made "coats of skins and clothed them."

So it is today. If we try to come to God dressed in our works of righteousness, we can never make it, for "all our righteousnesses are as filthy rags" in the presence of a holy God. *He* must provide the clothing.

One day, when "the marriage of the Lamb is come," His bride must be "arrayed in fine linen, clean and white...the righteousness of saints." But this righteousness will be *His*, "for we are his workmanship, created in Christ Jesus unto good works." Therefore, we are exhorted to "put on thy beautiful garments" and be prepared to meet our King.

Scripture:
Isaiah 61:10; 64:6; 52:1; Genesis 3:7,21;
Revelation 19:7-8; Ephesians 2:10

Springtime

Lo, the winter is past.

Many people welcome the spring after a heavy winter. This is true even for countries in temperate latitudes such as Israel, and it was just as real in Solomon's day as in ours.

In Solomon's Song of Songs, his new bride has been awaiting the spring return of her husband, who has been away during the winter. As she hears his call, she cries out, "Behold, he cometh," and then he arrives and says, "Rise up, my love, my fair one, and come away." "Lo, the winter is past."

This is also a beautiful allegory of Christ and His bride, the church, in which the winter is the long separation time between His ascension and His second coming. As He returns, we rise to meet and join Him in a glorious reunion. This scene may foreshadow the rapture of the church when Christ returns.

One cannot press allegories too far, but the wonderful promise of His return is no mere romantic story. "I will come again," He has assured us, "that where I am, there ye may be also" in that wonderful springtime of the coming of His kingdom.

Scripture:

Song of Solomon 2:8-13; 1 Thessalonians 4:16-17; John 14:3

The Camels Are Coming

Isaac…lifted up his eyes, and saw, and,
behold, the camels were coming.

Abraham commanded his eldest servant, Eliezer, to find a wife for his son Isaac. The servant saddled up camels and departed toward Mesopotamia.

Eliezer prayed for God's direction, "and it came to pass, before he had done speaking, that, behold, Rebekah came out." He followed her to her father's house and related the purpose of his visit. "And they called Rebekah, and said unto her, Wilt thou go with this man? And she said, I will go."

By God's providential direction, they knew the relationship was His will. "And the servant told Isaac all things that he had done. And Isaac brought her into his mother Sarah's tent, and took Rebekah, and she became his wife; and he loved her."

More than a romantic story, these events portray the evangelistic task of every believer. Like Eliezer, we are commanded by the Father to find a bride for His Son. As we seek to obey the Great Commission, we must pray for God's direction to the appropriate individuals who are prepared for a relationship with Christ. Lastly, we must point them to the wonderful Groom and rejoice to see them fall in love with Him.

Scripture:
Genesis 24:15,58,63,66-67

The Family in God's Plan

*I know him, that he will command his children
and his household after him, and they shall keep
the way of the LORD, to do justice and judgment.*

A family is the place to practice obedience.

God told the first man and woman to have children.
When the world filled with wickedness, He saved Noah's family and told them again to "be fruitful and multiply." When people rebelled against Him again, He led Abraham's family out to preserve them. Later, the Promised Land was divided according to families. Even Jesus was born into a family. The God who created the whole universe submitted to His parents!

When Jesus prioritized relationship with Himself over relationship with family, he was referring to salvation, not service. Christian workers are not to put their ministry before their family; ministry begins *with* the family.

The church is treated as a family. They met in homes. We are brothers and sisters in Christ. And one day, the Lamb will marry His bride, the church, and this family will live together forever.

Scripture:

Genesis 18:19; 1:27-28; 9:7; 12:1-3; Numbers 33:54;
Luke 2:51; Matthew 10:37-38

Love from the Beginning

*This is the message that ye heard from the
beginning, that we should love one another.*

Christ's command to love one another was new, but it has also been with us from the beginning: "Brethren, I write no new commandment unto you, but an old commandment which ye had from the beginning. The old commandment is the word which ye have heard from the beginning."

This is the same beginning as in Genesis 1:1 and John 1:1 and shown in 1 John: "That which was from the beginning... of the Word of life...that eternal life, which was with the Father, and was manifested unto us..."

"Let that therefore abide in you, which ye have heard from the beginning. If that which ye have heard from the beginning shall remain in you, ye also shall continue in the Son, and in the Father." This is an eternal commandment, for "God is love" and "love is of God."

Love has been at the center of God's plan from the beginning, but Christ gave a new pattern and measure of that love: "A new commandment I give unto you...as I have loved you... love one another."

Scripture:
1 John 3:11; 2:7,24; 1:1-2; 4:16,7; John 13:34

Love Your Enemies

I say unto you, love your enemies.

The command to love our enemies presumes that we will have enemies.

Jesus told this to His disciples, not to the multitude. "If the world hate you, ye know that it hated me before it hated you…If they have persecuted me, they will also persecute you."

He even called such persecution a blessing: "Blessed are they which are persecuted for righteousness' sake." "If ye be reproached for the name of Christ, happy are ye…But let none of you suffer as a murderer, or as a thief, or as an evildoer, or as a busybody in other men's matters. Yet if any man suffer as a Christian, let him not be ashamed; but let him glorify God on this behalf."

We can love our enemies only as we follow the example of Christ, "who, when he was reviled, reviled not again; when he suffered, he threatened not; but committed himself to him that judgeth righteously." "Therefore if thine enemy hunger, feed him; if he thirst, give him drink…Be not overcome of evil, but overcome evil with good."

Scripture:

Matthew 5:44,1,10; John 15:18,20; 1 Peter 4:14-16; 2:21,23; Romans 12:20-21

The "I Wills" of Christ

*Jesus, moved with compassion, put forth
his hand, and touched him, and saith
unto him, I will; be thou clean.*

When Jesus made the promise to the leper in Mark 1, "immediately the leprosy departed from him." The fulfillment of Jesus' promises may not always come as rapidly, but they will come.

"Follow me, and *I will* make you fishers of men," He promises all those who follow Him. But first they must come to Him and receive this promise: "Him that cometh to me *I will* in no wise cast out." Also, He promised, "Come unto me, all ye that labor and are heavy laden, and *I will* give you rest."

He also promised, "Whatsoever ye shall ask in my name, that *will I* do, that the Father may be glorified in the Son." And He promised to come back: "And if I go and prepare a place for you, *I will* come again, and receive you unto myself."

But probably the greatest of all His promises is this: "Father, *I will* that they also, whom thou hast given me, be with me where I am; that they may behold my glory."

Scripture:

Mark 1:41-42; Matthew 4:19; 11:28; John 6:37; 14:3,13; 17:24

The Togetherness of Believers

Can two walk together, except they be agreed?

Christians disagree on all sorts of things, and it is indeed difficult to walk together when we disagree so much on how to get where we want to go.

Nevertheless, Scripture exhorts that we be "together in the likeness of his death" and reveals that we were "quickened together," we were "raised up together," and we even "sit together in heavenly places in Christ Jesus." Furthermore, when Christ returns, we shall "be also glorified together."

Since we begin and end up together, it would seem we ought also to walk together, at least in spiritual agreement.

This is especially true of Christian husbands and wives. "What therefore God hath joined together, let not man put asunder." They are to be "heirs together of the grace of life." But this unity should also be true of the whole Christian family. Our hearts should be "knit together in love," and we should "stand fast in one spirit, with one mind striving together for the faith of the gospel." Finally, as "workers together with him," we should be "helping together by prayer."

Scripture:

Amos 3:3; Romans 6:5; 8:17; Ephesians 2:5-6;
Matthew 19:6; 1 Peter 3:7; Colossians 2:2; Philippians 1:27;
2 Corinthians 6:1; 1:11

Seeking Worshippers

The hour cometh, and now is, when the true worshippers shall worship the Father in spirit and in truth: for the Father seeketh such to worship him.

Here is an amazing revelation—the omnipotent God of creation actually seeks those among His creatures who would freely come to love and worship Him! How could He possibly have to seek anything? Yet Jesus said He does! In some inscrutable way, God's infinite heart is satisfied when we respond to His sacrificial love in gratitude and worship.

We see this also in the experience of the ten lepers. All ten had been cleansed of their leprosy, but only one, a Samaritan, returned to give thanks to Jesus. Note the wistfulness in Jesus' reply to the cleansed leper: "Were there not ten cleansed? but where are the nine? There are not found that returned to give glory to God, save this stranger." The Lord indeed takes note both of the few who truly appreciate Him and also of the many who take His blessings for granted.

Regardless of whether we fully understand, the Lord does seek those who will worship Him in spirit and in truth. Therefore, "Seek ye first the kingdom of God, and His righteousness; and all these things shall be added unto you."

Scripture:

John 4:23; Luke 17:17-18; Matthew 6:33

Judging One Another

There is one lawgiver, who is able to save and
to destroy: who art thou that judgest another?

We commit two types of sins related to criticism. We criticize others, and we take offense when others criticize us. To criticize is to judge, and as our text brings out, no one but God is qualified to judge. "Let us not therefore judge one another any more."

Criticism almost inevitably generates resentment, quarreling, and enmity. It actually harms the character and testimony of the critic as much as that of the recipient. Even unspoken criticism is harmful. Love "seeketh not her own, is not easily provoked, thinketh no evil."

This does not mean that Christians should condone doctrinal error or moral evil. "Judge not according to the appearance, but judge righteous judgment."

Others often criticize us. What should we do then? The answer is difficult to obey, but here it is: "For even hereunto were ye called: because Christ also suffered for us, leaving us an example, that ye should follow his steps…Who, when he was reviled, reviled not again; when he suffered, he threatened not; but committed himself to him that judgeth righteously."

Scripture:
James 4:12; Romans 14:13; 1 Corinthians 13:5;
John 7:24; 1 Peter 2:21-23

Magnificent Obsession

*Though I be free from all men, yet have I made
myself servant unto all, that I might gain the more.*

In his letter to the Ephesians, Paul noted that Christ had given specific gifts to the church—apostles, prophets, evangelists, pastors, and teachers. Paul himself was all of these, however, and he wanted to win as many people as he could from all walks of life. He therefore sought to be "made all things to all men, that [he] might by all means save some."

This, indeed, was a magnificent obsession, and every Christian should seek to emulate it as the Lord enables. Paul was not saying, however, that a man should become as a woman to win women to the Lord, or that a woman should become as a man to win men; neither should someone become a humanist to win humanists. One should never dilute the doctrines of the faith or Christian standards of conduct in order to win commitments to the church.

Paul was not laying down guidelines for witnessing, either for the church or for individual Christians. Rather, he was giving his own personal testimony. Nevertheless, we should seek to be understanding and sympathetic to people of every background.

Scripture:
1 Corinthians 9:19,22; Ephesians 4:11-16

The Cleansing Blood

*The blood of Jesus Christ his Son
cleanseth us from all sin.*

A common cultic heresy asserts that the blood of Christ has no cleansing efficacy of itself, but this contradicts the plain statement of our text. John wrote those words long after Christ's blood had all been spilled on the cross, but it was still miraculously cleansing sinners in his day and is in ours as well.

Christ's blood supported His physical life, for "the life of the flesh is in the blood." But His blood was not like the blood of other men, for it was "the precious blood of Christ, as of a lamb without blemish and without spot." It was uncontaminated, either by genetic defects due to accumulated generations of mutations (as in all other men and women) or by inherent sin.

When His blood was shed, it did not simply disappear into the ground and decay into dust, any more than did His body in the tomb, for it had been an integral part of His perfect human body, which was to be raised and glorified.

As our great high priest, Jesus somehow took the atoning blood into the holy place in the heavenly tabernacle.

Scripture:
1 John 1:7; Leviticus 17:11; 1 Peter 1:19

Always Rejoicing

Rejoice evermore.

Most people think that John 11:35 ("Jesus wept") is the shortest verse in the Bible, but our text is actually even shorter in the original Greek.

In one sense, these two two-word verses complement each other. Because Jesus wept, we can rejoice evermore. Christ died that we might live. He became poor so that we could be eternally rich. When Christ rose from the dead and met the women returning from the empty tomb, He greeted them by saying, "All hail." The Greek word Matthew uses is the same word that is often translated "rejoice," and surely Jesus' victory over sin and death provided the greatest of all reasons for the world to rejoice.

The contrast between suffering and rejoicing is present throughout the New Testament, and suffering typically precedes and brings in the rejoicing. The contrast first occurs in the closing verse of the beatitudes: "Blessed are ye, when men shall revile you, and persecute you…for my sake. Rejoice, and be exceeding glad: for great is your reward in heaven."

In that great day, "God shall wipe away all tears from their eyes," and all the redeemed will indeed rejoice evermore.

Scripture:
1 Thessalonians 5:16; Matthew 28:9; 5:11-12;
Revelation 19:7; 21:4

Let Him Hear

He that hath ears to hear, let him hear.

The Lord Jesus Christ must have considered this exhortation to be of great importance, for He pronounces it eight times in the four Gospels and seven times in Revelation. John apparently uttered it once himself.

It is urgent, therefore, that people hear God's Word not only with their ears but also with understanding minds, believing hearts, and obedient lives.

First of all, unsaved men and women must respond to the gospel message in this way. Jesus said, "Verily, verily, I say unto you, he that heareth my word, and believeth on him that sent me, hath everlasting life, and shall not come into condemnation, but is passed from death unto life." Hearing this message with believing minds and hearts means all the difference between heaven and hell.

But that's just the beginning. Jesus also said, "My sheep hear my voice, and I know them, and they follow me: and I give unto them eternal life; and they shall never perish, neither shall any man pluck them out of my hand."

Scripture:
Matthew 11:15; Revelation 13:9; John 5:24; 10:27-28

Mortified

If ye live after the flesh, ye shall die: but
if ye through the Spirit do mortify the
deeds of the body, ye shall live.

To mortify something means to put it to death. Paul taught in our text and in other passages that the "deeds of the body," or its fleshly actions and appetites—all that pertains to "the old man"—should be mortified, or put to death.

This mortification is first of all judicial. Christ has been put to death in our stead. "Our old man is crucified with him, that the body of sin be destroyed, that henceforth we should not serve sin."

But the mortification must not stop there, with only a positional death. It must also be an actual mortification in practice, for "they that are Christ's have crucified the flesh with its affections and lusts. If we live in the Spirit, let us also walk in the Spirit."

"For as ye have yielded your members' servants to uncleanness and to iniquity unto iniquity; even so now yield your members' servants to righteousness unto holiness."

The choice is clear! It will be either death to the flesh or death to the Spirit.

Scripture:
Romans 8:13; 6:6,19; Galatians 5:24-25

Hiding from God

There is nothing covered, that shall not be revealed; and hid, that shall not be known.

The psalmist knew that hiding from God was a fruitless enterprise. "Whither shall I go from thy Spirit? or whither shall I flee from thy presence?" He also knew (and described in various graphic passages, such as Psalm 51) that his sin drove him to hide from God and erected a wall of separation between him and God.

It has never been any different. The very first human sin led the very first humans to hide from God. "They heard the voice of the LORD God walking in the garden in the cool of the day: and Adam and his wife hid themselves from the presence of the LORD God amongst the trees of the garden."

"O God, thou knowest my foolishness; and my sins are not hid from thee."

How much better to acknowledge and repent of our sins, and say with David, "Hide thy face from my sins, and blot out all mine iniquities. Create in me a clean heart, O God; and renew a right spirit within me."

Scripture:

Matthew 10:26; Psalm 139:7; 51:9-10; 69:5; Genesis 3:8

Things to Flee

Flee also youthful lusts.

Some things are so fearful and deadly that to try to face them at all is foolish. The only rational course, when confronted by them, is to flee!

The most obvious of all such enemies is the wrath of God, for His judgment is terrible and eternal. His message is to "flee from the wrath to come" by receiving Christ as Savior.

Certain sins have such deadly consequences, even in this present life, that the Scriptures warn us to flee from them. "O man of God, flee these things." In context, the apostle Paul is warning against "the love of money." Those who desire to be rich, he says, "fall into temptation and a snare, and into many foolish and hurtful lusts, which drown men in destruction and perdition."

He also warns us to "flee from idolatry"—that is, from worshipping and serving any part of the creation "more than the Creator."

We must "flee fornication," a deadly danger to the Christian in this day of immorality. Finally, as our text says, young believers should "flee also youthful lusts" so we can "call on the Lord out of a pure heart."

Scripture:
2 Timothy 2:22; Matthew 3:7; 1 Timothy 6:5-11;
1 Corinthians 6:18; 10:14; Romans 1:25

Sign of the Sabbath

It is a sign between me and the children
of Israel for ever: for in six days the LORD
made heaven and earth, and on the seventh
day he rested, and was refreshed.

"Sabbath" means "rest" (not "seventh"), and God, in His omniscience, knew that we would need a day of rest and remembrance of Him as Creator if we were to serve Him effectively. "The Sabbath was made for man," said the Lord Jesus.

This is why the weekly day of rest and worship was to be a sign forever, and also probably why breaking the Sabbath was a capital crime for God's covenant people, Israel. "Six days may work be done; but in the seventh is the sabbath of rest, holy to the LORD: whosoever doeth any work in the sabbath day, he shall surely be put to death."

This severe penalty may no longer apply today, but it does indicate the importance God placed on His week of creation. Just as the rainbow was the sign of His covenant with the world through Noah, and circumcision the sign of His covenant with the seed of Abraham, so a weekly day of worship is the sign that we still honor Him as our Creator and Savior.

Scripture:
Exodus 31:15,17; Mark 2:27

Be Fruitful and Multiply

God blessed them, and God said unto them, Be
fruitful, and multiply, and replenish the earth.

This was God's very first command to the first man and
woman, and it applies to the whole earth. To subdue the
earth implies the development of science and technology,
commerce and education—indeed, every honorable human
vocation.

As God's first "great commission," it applies to all people and has never been withdrawn. God even expanded it to
Noah after the Flood, twice repeating the command to "be
fruitful and multiply." In order to really subdue and exercise
dominion over the earth, a large population would be necessary, and as such God's command has never yet been fully
accomplished. Vast areas of the earth are still barren and unde-
veloped.

Jesus said to His disciples, "I have chosen you, and
ordained you, that ye should go and bring forth fruit, and
that your fruit should remain." That is, we who are His disciples are to be fruitful and multiply spiritually as well. Then, in
the age to come, the first great mandate will also finally be fulfilled, "for the earth shall be full of the knowledge of the LORD,
as the waters cover the sea."

Scripture:

Genesis 1:28; 9:1-7; John 15:16; Isaiah 11:9

The Peacemaker

…having made peace through the blood of his
cross, by him to reconcile all things unto himself.

Is it possible for us to make peace with God? No! The only
one who can make peace between spiritually dead sinners
and God is God Himself, for only the living God can bring
life out of death.

Jesus Christ is the only true Peacemaker, for He "made
peace" between sinful, spiritually dead men and women and
the living, holy God, and He could only do it through "the
blood of his cross." The Lord Jesus Himself has made this crys-
tal clear. "Peace I leave with you, my peace I give unto you: not
as the world giveth, give I unto you." He had to die for our
sins before we could ever be reconciled to God. "These things
I have spoken unto you, that in me ye might have peace. In the
world ye shall have tribulation: but be of good cheer; I have
overcome the world."

He is our great Peacemaker, and we receive that peace
when we receive Him. "Being justified by faith, we have peace
with God through our Lord Jesus Christ."

Scripture:
Colossians 1:20; Matthew 5:9; John 14:27; 16:33;
Romans 5:1

The Unseen Angels

He shall give his angels charge over
thee, to keep thee in all thy ways.

God has created "an innumerable company of angels," but few living men or women have ever actually seen real heavenly angels. We may "have entertained angels unawares," for they can assume the appearance of men on occasion, but normally they are invisible to human eyes.

Furthermore, they are "all ministering spirits, sent forth to minister for them who shall be heirs of salvation." God has given them charge over us—that is, over each believer "that dwelleth in the secret place of the most High."

Wide is the variety of His commands with respect to angelic ministry to believers. "The angel of the LORD encampeth round about them that fear him, and delivereth them… They shall bear thee up in their hands, lest thou dash thy foot against a stone."

Angels are keenly concerned with our salvation and spiritual progress, "which things the angels desire to look into." Finally, "when the Son of man shall come in his glory," He will bring "all the holy angels with him" as He judges the world.

Scripture:
Psalm 91:1,11-12; 34:7; Hebrews 12:22; 13:2; 1:14;
1 Peter 1:12; Matthew 5:31

The Fight of Faith

Fight the good fight of faith, lay hold on eternal life, whereunto thou art also called, and hast professed a good profession before many witnesses.

Faith is the *door* by which men and women enter the family of the redeemed. Paul reported how God "had opened the door of faith unto the Gentiles." Those who enter become a "household of faith." "The just shall live by faith."

Faith is also *work*. "Remembering without ceasing your work of faith" is vital, because "faith without works is dead."

Furthermore, there is *a fight* of faith. The Christian is constantly under attack by the devil, and only through faith can he stand. "Let us, who are of the day, be sober, putting on the breastplate of faith and love."

Let us, therefore, like Abraham, be "strong in faith, giving glory to God." Our faith is well placed, for it centers on Christ, the mighty Creator, living Savior, and coming King, who is author of the wonderful "word of faith, which we preach."

Scripture:

1 Timothy 6:12; Acts 14:27; Galatians 6:10; 3:11;
1 Thessalonians 1:3; 5:8; James 2:20; Romans 4:20; 10:8

Created, Formed, Made

…even every one that is called by my name:
for I have created him for my glory, I have
formed him; yea, I have made him.

There are three main verbs used to describe God's work of creation in Genesis—"create" (Hebrew *bara*), "make" (*asah*), and "form" (*yatsar*). They are similar in meaning, but each has a slightly different emphasis, and not one of them ever suggests the idea of evolution.

All three verbs are used in Genesis with reference to man. "And God said, Let us *make* man in our image…So God *created* man in his own image…And the LORD God *formed* man of the dust of the ground."

Creation is the first significant topic in Genesis, but it is mentioned even more frequently in Isaiah. The words *bara* and *yatsar* are used twice as often in Isaiah as in any other Old Testament book, and the words are applied uniquely to works of God.

God created, formed, made, and established the earth, that it might be the home of men and women. But what was God's purpose for the people who would inhabit it? "I have created him…I have formed him…I have made him…for my glory."

Scripture:

Isaiah 43:7; Genesis 1:26-27; 2:7

Arrogance

The fear of the LORD is to hate evil: pride,
and arrogancy, and the evil way.

Few things are more abominable to God than arrogance. When the prophet Isaiah saw the daughters of Israel walking in contemptuous pride, he said, "Moreover the LORD saith, Because the daughters of Zion are haughty, and walk with stretched forth necks and wanton eyes, walking and mincing as they go, and making a tinkling with their feet: Therefore the LORD will smite…the daughters of Zion."

Several chapters later Isaiah declares the sure judgment awaiting the arrogant. "I will cause the arrogancy of the proud to cease, and will lay low the haughtiness of the terrible." Solomon also says, "Pride goeth before destruction, and an haughty spirit before a fall."

The cure for arrogance is repentance. In contrast to the condemnation Isaiah spoke against those who walked arrogantly, he announced God's promise: "I dwell in the high and holy place, with him also that is of a contrite and humble spirit, to revive the spirit of the humble, and to revive the heart of the contrite ones."

God is quick to extend mercy to the contrite, but He has no patience for the arrogance of sinful man.

Scripture:
Proverbs 8:13; 16:18; Isaiah 3:16-17; 13:11; 57:15

Unto Me

He that oppresseth the poor reproacheth his Maker:
but he that honoreth him hath mercy on the poor.

Jesus said, "Inasmuch as ye have done it unto one of the least of these my brethren, ye have done it unto me." The Lord taught that our attitude in helping the needy is to be one of gladly giving or ministering to Him. Even unpleasant kindnesses done as to the Lord makes any act sweet.

Remember Abraham of old, who took in three wandering strangers? He killed a calf and prepared a feast for them under the tree. Afterward he realized that two of his guests were angels and that the other was the Lord.

How many times have we turned away a needy one without so much as a look of kindness? Could it be that Jesus Christ comes to us periodically, knocking on our door or holding out His hand? How can we recognize Him? Only by faith, believing that what He said was true: "If you do it to them, you do it to me."

May the Lord remind us at such times to minister lovingly to those He sends our way.

Scripture:
Proverbs 14:31; Matthew 25:40; Genesis 18:1-16

The Witness of Conscience

They which heard it, being convicted by their
own conscience, went out one by one.

This is the first of 32 occurrences of the word "conscience" in the New Testament. By pricking the consciences of an angry mob, Jesus prevented the accusers from stoning a woman charged with adultery. Those who had been quick to judge suddenly recognized their own unworthiness to do so.

A conscience can be a reliable guide, however, only if it is a good conscience. On the other hand, the Scriptures speak of those who have a "weak conscience," which may become a "defiled conscience" and eventually a "seared conscience" or even an "evil conscience."

What makes a conscience good? Exercise. In Paul's testimony before Felix, he stated, "And herein do I exercise myself, to have always a conscience void of offense toward God, and toward men." The "exercise" (literally, "training") that had produced such a conscience in Paul, he said, was the Word of God. A lifelong study of the Scriptures, accompanied by absolute faith in their veracity and authority, had produced in Paul a strong, pure, good, and reliable conscience, and it will do the same for us.

Scripture:
John 8:9; 1 Corinthians 8:7,10,12; Titus 1:15;
1 Timothy 4:2; Hebrews 10:22; Acts 24:16

The Watchers

*This matter is by the decree of the watchers, and
the demand by the word of the holy ones.*

"The watchers" are mentioned in the Bible only here in the
fourth chapter of Daniel, all three times evidently synon-
ymous with "the holy ones"—beings who come down from
heaven. Such phrases could apply only to angels, created to
serve the Lord and the "heirs of salvation."

The word is used in reference to Nebuchadnezzar's vision
and period of insanity. The Bible indicates that "the angels
desire to look into" the outworking of the gospel in the hearts
of men. Paul said that God gave him grace to preach so that
"unto the principalities and powers in heavenly places might
be known by the church the manifold wisdom of God." Children as well as adult believers seem to have guardian angels
who "watch" them.

This is a mysterious subject because we cannot see these
"watchers," but we at least need to know they are there. In fact,
we can praise God that "the angel of the Lord encampeth
round about them that fear him, and delivereth them."

Scripture:
Daniel 4:17; 1 Peter 1:12; Ephesians 3:10; Matthew 18:10;
Acts 12:9,15; Psalm 34:7

An Early Confession

*Without controversy great is the
mystery of godliness.*

A "mystery" in Scripture is something that was previously hidden but is now revealed. Here the mystery is the blessed truth that God is in the business of producing godliness in the lives of men and women. Paul used a doctrinal confession, or hymn, to describe this mystery.

1. *"God was manifest in the flesh, justified in the Spirit."* This couplet relates Christ's human-divine nature. His humanity was evident to all; His divinity was declared through the Spirit.

2. *"...seen of angels, preached unto the Gentiles."* Angels observed, and to some degree, participated in Christ's earthly ministry, but the salvation and godliness He offered was only to men, "which things the angels desire to look into."

3. *"...believed on in the world, received up into glory."* Other teachers have gained a following, but only Christ ascended directly into heaven following His resurrection.

Doctrinal confessions or hymns can help us learn and remember truth, but the goal of each is godliness—"this mystery among the Gentiles; which is Christ in you."

Scripture:
1 Timothy 3:16; Colossians 1:27; 1 Peter 1:12

211

Bruising the Devil

*The God of peace shall bruise Satan
under your feet shortly.*

This promise is a clear allusion to the primeval assurance of Genesis 3:15, when God promised that the unique "seed" of "the woman" would eventually "bruise" (actually "crush") the head of the serpent, the devil. This prophecy will finally be fulfilled in Christ's ultimate victory, when Satan first will be bound for a thousand years in the bottomless pit and then confined forever in the lake of fire.

In the meantime believers can repeatedly achieve local and temporary victories over Satan by resisting him. God promises that if we resist him as Jesus did, he will flee. The ultimate victory over Satan, of course, will be won only by the Lord Jesus when He returns, and we must "be sober, be vigilant" until that time.

Whether we are aware of it or not, we must perpetually "wrestle…against the rulers of the darkness of this world," who cast "fiery darts" against each believer. Finally, with the sword of the Spirit, which is the Word of God, we can even by God's grace inflict spiritual wounds on Satan himself.

Scripture:
Romans 16:20; Revelation 20:2,10; 1 Peter 5:8-9;
James 4:7; Ephesians 6:12-17

I Will Guide Thee with Mine Eye

I will instruct thee and teach thee
in the way which thou shalt go: I
will guide thee with mine eye.

Psalm 32 is the first of the 14 psalms that are headed by the title *Maschil*, or "instruction." These 14 psalms occur in the following symmetrical pattern: one of them in book 1 of the Psalms; four each in books 2, 3, and 4; and one in book 5.

This psalm contains David's personal testimony of intense soul-searing conviction following his awful sin in the matter of Bathsheba—adultery and murder.

God's "hand was heavy" on David until finally he says, "I acknowledged my sin unto thee...thou forgavest the iniquity of my sin." Once a sinning saint has come to God in confession and true repentance, there is indeed real forgiveness and cleansing, and the happiness of salvation is restored.

God desires his children not to be "as the horse, or as the mule" that have to be guided forcibly, but to be so in tune with His Word and His will that He can guide them gently and quietly, like a mother who directs an obedient and loving child merely by the look in her eye. The happy life is one of obedience to the guiding eye of the Lord.

Scripture:
Psalm 32:3-5,8-9

Why the Righteous Suffer

I have heard of thee by the hearing of the
ear: but now mine eye seeth thee. Wherefore I
abhor myself, and repent in dust and ashes.

After a fruitful life of great prosperity and high esteem in the community, Job suddenly lost all his possessions, all his children, his health, his wife's love, and his closest friends' respect. His friends, presuming to defend God's character, insisted that Job must have been guilty of some terrible secret sin. But Job, in all good conscience, while still trusting God, felt he had to defend his own integrity against these false charges.

Nevertheless, when Job encountered God Himself, he could only despise his own proud self-righteousness and prostrate himself in dust and ashes. In the presence of God, even the most holy among men appear vile, and the sin of pride must somehow be purged before they are fully like Jesus.

This is why Job and Daniel and Paul and all other godly men and women must suffer in some degree as training for heavenly service. "Unto you it is given in the behalf of Christ, not only to believe on him, but also to suffer for his sake."

Scripture:
Job 42:5-6; 1:8; Philippians 1:29

The Bringing Forth

Therefore will he give them up, until the time
that she which travaileth hath brought forth.

This enigmatic verse must be understood in the light of its context. The verse preceding it is the great Christmas verse: "Thou, Bethlehem Ephratah...out of thee shall he come forth unto me that is to be ruler in Israel; whose goings forth have been from of old, from everlasting."

The verse following today's text says, "He shall stand and feed in the strength of the LORD, in the majesty of the name of the LORD his God; and they shall abide: for now shall he be great unto the ends of the earth."

There was a babe born in Bethlehem who has been "going forth" forever. He is also to "come forth" unto God, but not until a woman in travail has "brought forth." Once He does come forth, He is to restore and rule Israel, yet be great unto the ends of the earth.

Ever since Eve, "she which travaileth" must "bring forth children" in sorrow, and the "mighty God," whose "goings forth have been from everlasting," must become a child, "made of a woman," destroying the serpent so that all who trust in Him "shall abide" forever.

Scripture:
Micah 5:2-4; Genesis 3:16; Galatians 4:4

Chastening

Behold, happy is the man whom God
correcteth: therefore despise not thou
the chastening of the Almighty.

True parental love requires appropriate chastening, and chastening, rightly received, generates blessing and happiness. "He that spareth his rod hateth his son: but he that loveth him chasteneth him betimes." This is effective child rearing, assuming that the chastening is remedial rather than vindictive and is applied in love rather than anger. But the main teaching of such passages goes beyond parental child-training methods to the grand theme of God's spiritual training of His children for eternity.

This thought is often expressed in the Psalms, but it is especially clear in the Proverbs. "My son, despise not the chastening of the LORD; neither be weary of his correction: for whom the LORD loveth he correcteth; even as a father the son in whom he delighteth."

The classic passage on this theme is in Hebrews, which begins by quoting the above verses in Proverbs and then concludes, "No chastening for the present seemeth to be joyous, but grievous: nevertheless afterward it yieldeth the peaceable fruit of righteousness unto them which are exercised thereby."

Scripture:
Job 5:17; Proverbs 13:24; 3:11-12; Hebrews 12:11;
Revelation 3:19

The Creator's Hands

In his hand are the deep places of the earth…
and his hands formed the dry land.

When the Creator walked on the earth, He put His hands on the blind man of Bethsaida and restored the man's sight. This was not an isolated incident. "When the sun was setting he laid his hands on every one of them, and healed them."

The creative hands of the Lord Jesus extend to every aspect of creation: "Thou, Lord, in the beginning hast laid the foundation of the earth; and the heavens are the works of thine hands."

His hands also became engraved, eventually nailed to a cross according to divine plan. God had previously asked, "Can a woman forget her suckling child, that she should not have compassion on the son of her womb?" He blessed children, placing hands on them, and reached out from glory to touch a trembling disciple. He holds disciples today in His hand, affirming, "Neither shall any man pluck them out of my hand."

He will return with uplifted hands too, for the Scripture reads, "This same Jesus, which is taken up…shall so come in like manner as ye have seen him go into heaven."

Scripture:

Psalm 95:4-5; Mark 8:23-25; Luke 4:40; Hebrews 1:8,10;
Psalm 22:16; Isaiah 49:15; Revelation 1:17; John 10:28; Acts 1:11

Christ the Creationist

In those days shall be affliction, such as
was not from the beginning of the creation
which God created unto this time.

In predicting a future judgment on the world, the Lord Jesus referred to "the beginning of the creation which God created," thus affirming the biblical doctrine of supernatural, sudden creation. Evolutionary ideas were dominant almost everywhere in Jesus' day. The Epicureans, for example, were atheistic evolutionists. But Christ was a creationist, and the much maligned creation scientists of today are following His example and teaching.

Speaking of Adam and Eve, Jesus affirmed that "from the beginning of the creation God made them male and female." The pagans all believed in an eternal cosmos, but Jesus said that it had a beginning and that man and woman were a part of that beginning creation.

He also believed that the two parts of the account of creation (Genesis 1 and 2) were complimentary, not contradictory. "Have ye not read," He said, referring to Genesis 1, "that he which made them at the beginning made them male and female?" And referring to Genesis 2, He said, "For this cause shall a man leave father and mother, and shall cleave to his wife: and they twain shall be one flesh."

Scripture:
Mark 13:19; 10:6; 2:27; Matthew 19:4-6

Cursed Is the Ground

Cursed is the ground for thy sake; in sorrow
shalt thou eat of it all the days of thy life.

The great curse that God placed on the ground because of man's rebellion is global. Until sin is removed, the curse will remain. "The whole creation groaneth and travaileth in pain together until now."

Plants and animals, men and women, minerals and mountains…all may grow for a time, but all eventually decay and die because God's curse is in the very dust of the ground from which they are formed. The principle has even come to be recognized by scientists as the law of entropy, which has no known exception.

In the new earth, however, when Christ returns to reign in glory and all unrepentant, unbelieving sinners have been cast with Satan into the lake of fire, "there shall be no more curse." The whole creation "shall be delivered from the bondage of corruption into the glorious liberty of the children of God."

Therefore, "we, according to his promise, look for new heavens and a new earth, wherein dwelleth righteousness."

Scripture:

Genesis 3:17; Revelation 22:3; Romans 8:21-22; 2 Peter 3:13

Forsake and Follow

When they had brought their ships to
land, they forsook all, and followed him.

The word "forsook" indicates that the disciples completely severed themselves from their own situations and relationships. They gave up everything for Jesus. For Peter, James, John, and Andrew, this involved leaving a prosperous business; for Matthew, a prestigious position of wealth. Certainly each left his livelihood, security, training, possessions, relationships, hopes—everything. "Whosoever he be of you that forsaketh not all that he hath, he cannot be my disciple." The other disciples also restructured their lives and loyalties to those of Christ.

The word "follow" implies a unity of purpose and direction. Jesus told the rich young ruler to give up all vestiges of his materialistic life "and come, take up the cross, and follow me."

Peter asked Jesus the question that we frequently ask. "Behold, we have forsaken all, and followed thee; what shall we have therefore?" Christ answered, "Every one that hath forsaken houses, or brethren, or sisters, or father, or mother, or wife, or children, or lands, for my name's sake, shall receive an hundredfold, and shall inherit everlasting life."

Scripture:

Luke 5:10-11; 14:33; Matthew 27:50; 19:27,29; Mark 10:21

By Nature

...and were by nature the children of wrath.

Many Christians are under the mistaken notion that children are innocent, but the Scriptures teach differently: "The LORD said in his heart, I will not again curse the ground any more for man's sake; for the imagination of man's heart is evil from his youth." David said, "Behold, I was shapen in iniquity; and in sin did my mother conceive me." Our text indicates that we are "by nature the children of wrath."

When do we ever have to teach children to be selfish and disobedient? It comes naturally—like weeds in a garden. The real task is teaching children to be others-centered, honest, and obedient. True, they have the desirable quality of trustfulness, and the Lord would have us trust Him similarly. But this does not mean that children are innocent.

The Bible gives the bad news about our nature, but it also presents the good news about the love and mercy of our God. Some parents may hold off telling their children about sin and their need for Jesus until they think they really need Him. The fact is, however, that children need this knowledge from the start.

Scripture:

Ephesians 2:3; Genesis 8:21; Psalm 51:5

Little Children

Except ye be converted, and become
as little children, ye shall not enter
into the kingdom of heaven.

Are children too young to understand the gospel? Should we wait to teach them about Christ until they're older? Jesus taught that those who come to the Savior must become like little children before they can really comprehend the way of salvation and be converted. He also said, "Suffer little children to come unto me, and forbid them not: for of such is the kingdom of God."

A very young child can surely understand that God made him, that he sins against God when he does wrong, that God sent His Son, Jesus, to die for his sins, and that Jesus can save him and take him to heaven. An adult may require much explanation and may imagine many difficulties, but a child will simply believe—and that's enough!

The word for "little child" or "little children" actually means children who are not much more than toddlers. It is the same word rendered "young child" when the wise men came to find Jesus in Bethlehem.

Little children should, by all means, be taught the gospel and should be encouraged to come to Christ before they grow too old.

Scripture:
Matthew 18:2-3; Luke 18:16-17

Little Children

I write unto you, little children, because your
sins are forgiven you for his name's sake.

There are two main words for "children" in the New Testament. One, *paidon*, refers to young children. This is the word used by Jesus when he says, "Suffer little children, and forbid them not, to come unto me: for of such is the kingdom of heaven." The other word is *teknon* and points to the parent-child relationship. John predominantly uses *teknon* to embrace his relationship with the "sons of God" to whom he is addressing his letter.

A common salvation and forgiveness of sins, of course, are what make us related. John had just exhorted us not to sin, but if and when we do, our relationship with the Father provides the Advocate, Jesus Christ.

Yet John also notes that even as "little" children we had "known the Father." Perhaps this is an allusion to the great message written in the heavens or in the creation itself, or perhaps John refers to the foundational knowledge that such children would have heard from their parents. But it surely encompasses the simple truth that God "exists," from which all faith must begin. Even little children know that!

Scripture:
1 John 2:1,12-13; 3:2; Matthew 19:14; 18:3;
Romans 1:20; Hebrews 11:5

Christ and the Writings of Moses

Had ye believed Moses, ye would have believed me.

The Jewish leaders in Jesus' day always made a great show of allegiance to the teachings of Moses in the Pentateuch. But Jesus pointed out that this was hypocritical because Moses wrote of Him, yet they refused to believe His words.

Many Christian intellectuals today are involved in even greater hypocrisy, professing to believe in Christ while rejecting the plain teachings of Genesis and the other books of Moses. The Lord Jesus, for example, taught that "from the beginning of the creation God made them male and female," and also that therefore "shall a man leave his father and his mother, and shall cleave unto his wife: and they shall be one flesh."

These compromising Christians insist that He was quoting from two contradictory accounts of creation and that men and women were not at the beginning of creation, but came along about 4.5 billion years after the creation of the earth and about 15 billion years after the beginning of the cosmos.

Rejecting Moses and his teaching to their shame, how can they really believe in Christ when they reject His words?

Scripture:

John 5:46-47; Genesis 1:27; 2:24; Luke 17:26-27

Entertaining Angels

Be not forgetful to entertain strangers: for thereby
some have entertained angels unawares.

Angels are not human, they are spirits, "sent forth to minister for them who shall be heirs of salvation." But they can take on the actual appearance of men when the need arises. The allusion in our text to some who have unwittingly played host to angelic visitors probably refers to Abraham, who entertained God and two angels, appearing as men. Lot, down in Sodom, offered the hospitality of his home to these two angels that evening. Because of the wicked reputation of the Sodomites, these angels the next day enabled Lot and his daughters to escape.

Most of us have never seen an angel unless we, like Abraham and Lot, have unwittingly encountered them. But the marvelous fact is that they are there when needed. "The angel of the LORD encampeth round about them that fear him, and delivereth them." Daniel exclaimed, "My God hath sent his angel, and hath shut the lions' mouths, that they have not hurt me." God indeed is able to deliver us when we have a special need and when we call on Him in faith.

Scripture:
Hebrews 13:2; 1:14; Genesis 18:2; 19:24;
Psalm 34:7; Daniel 6:22

The Heart of Our Understanding

Brethren, be not children in understanding:
howbeit in malice be ye children, but
in understanding be men.

The wise man wrote, "With all thy getting get understanding." However, the understanding we acquire must not be perverted by the spirit of this world.

Writing to the Ephesians, Paul contrasted a darkened understanding and a spiritually illuminated understanding. "Walk not as other Gentiles walk in the vanity of their mind, having the understanding darkened, being alienated from the life of God through the ignorance that is in them, because of the blindness of their heart." A blinded heart produces a darkened understanding. Paul prayed that God would give them "the spirit of wisdom and revelation in the knowledge of him: the eyes of [their] understanding being enlightened." We need an understanding enlightened by the Holy Spirit, not darkened by a hardened heart.

We should seek a mature understanding of the things of God, not remaining stagnant at the elementary level of understanding. It is dishonoring to the Lord who called us into His family to remain spiritual children. "Grow in grace, and in the knowledge of our Lord and Savior Jesus Christ."

Scripture:
1 Corinthians 14:20; Proverbs 4:7;
Ephesians 4:17-18; 1:17-18; 2 Peter 3:18

Curiously Wrought

My substance was not hid from thee, when
I was made in secret, and curiously
wrought in the lowest parts of the earth.

This marvelous picture of an embryonic child growing in its mother's womb is scientifically accurate and shows clearly that God is concerned with the developing infant from the very moment of conception. "Thou hast covered me in my mother's womb." The child is "wonderfully made," designed to be like all human beings but unique in detail.

God was secretly making "my substance"—that is, the skeletal frame—and embroidering it ("curiously wrought") "in the lowest parts of the earth." This seems to be a remarkable anticipation of the double-helical DNA molecular program, which organizes the beautiful structure of the whole child.

"Substance, yet being unperfect" is one word in the Hebrew, meaning "embryo." All of its members were written in God's book before they existed—probably from the foundation of the world. Then He "fashioned" it (same word as when He "formed" Adam's body), and watched over it continually from then on.

Scripture:

Psalm 139:13-16; Genesis 2:7

Peace like a River

*The peace of God, which passeth all
understanding, shall keep your hearts
and minds through Christ Jesus.*

The beloved hymn "It is Well with My Soul" was written in memory of the author's four precious daughters, who had just perished in a shipwreck. His wife barely survived. Through it all, the couple maintained faith in their God and made this confession through their tears:

> When peace like a river, attendeth my way, /
> When sorrows like sea billows roll, / Whatever
> my lot, Thou hast taught me to say, / It is well,
> it is well, with my soul.

God has not promised a life of ease, free from heartache or tragedy, but He *has* promised to be with us. "Though I walk through the valley of the shadow of death, I will fear no evil: for thou art with me." There is a prerequisite for the "peace of God, which passeth all understanding": "Be careful [that is, anxious] for nothing; but in every thing by prayer and supplication with thanksgiving let your requests be made known unto God."

"Thou wilt keep him in perfect peace, whose mind is stayed on thee."

Scripture:
Philippians 4:6-7; Psalm 23:4; Isaiah 43:1-3; 26:3

The Christian's Calling

I therefore, the prisoner of the Lord,
beseech you that ye walk worthy of the
vocation wherewith ye are called.

The Christian's calling in Christ is a high calling, a worthy vocation.

Our calling is "of God" and irrevocable. We are called "by his grace" and "into the grace of Christ." We are called "out of darkness" and "into his marvelous light."

We are "called to be saints." He has "called us with an holy calling." We are "called unto the fellowship of his Son Jesus Christ our Lord." We are "called unto liberty."

We are called to suffer. "Hereunto were ye called: because Christ also suffered for us, leaving us an example, that ye should follow his steps." The "eternal life, whereunto thou art also called" may not come easily, for it involves the "good fight of faith."

We are called "to glory and virtue," even "his eternal glory by Christ Jesus," for we are "called the sons of God."

"Give diligence to make your calling and election sure."

Scripture:
Ephesians 4:1; Romans 11:29; 1:7; Galatians 1:6,15; 5:13;
1 Peter 2:9,21; 2 Timothy 1:9; 1 Corinthians 1:9;
1 Timothy 6:12; 1 John 3:1; 2 Peter 1:3,10

Heartfelt Prayer

Let us lift up our heart with our
hands unto God in the heavens.

The Lord Jesus cautioned us about insincere prayers: "When ye pray, use not vain repetitions, as the heathen do: for they think that they shall be heard for their much speaking."

Many people will lift their hands to pray or prostrate themselves on the ground. Some will stand, some will kneel. Some will write out their prayers and then read them to an audience; others will pray eloquently and at great length. But the thing that counts far more than posture or eloquence is our attitude of heart. We must lift up our hearts to the Lord, not just our hands or our voices.

We need to feel as the psalmist felt: "As the hart panteth after the water brooks, so panteth my soul after thee, O God." Our hearts need first to be right, of course—pure and true in His sight. "If I regard iniquity in my heart, the Lord will not hear me." We are to "call on the Lord out of a pure heart."

"The effectual fervent prayer of a righteous man availeth much."

Scripture:
Lamentations 3:41; Matthew 6:7-8; Psalm 42:1; 66:18;
2 Timothy 2:22; James 5:16

Watching for Christ's Return

*Watch therefore: for ye know not what
hour your Lord doth come.*

We don't know just when, but Christ *will* return, for so
He promised, and He can neither lie nor fail. He has
repeatedly made it plain that no one can determine the date
of His coming. Not even He, while in His human limitations,
knew that.

He did not tell us to watch for the antichrist or the revival
of Rome's empire or a great apostasy or a great revival or a
world government or anything else—just for Him! Note some
of His commands to do this: "Take ye heed, watch and pray,
for ye know not when the time is." "Watch ye therefore...lest
coming suddenly, he find you sleeping." "Watch therefore, for
ye know neither the day nor the hour wherein the Son of man
cometh."

In addition to such exhortations by the Lord Himself, the
apostles also sounded similar warnings. "Unto them that look
for him shall he appear the second time without sin unto salvation." "Abide in him; that, when he shall appear, we may have
confidence, and not be ashamed before him at his coming."

Scripture:
Matthew 24:42; 25:13; Mark 13:32-36;
Hebrews 9:28; 1 John 2:28

Judgment in the New Testament

...in flaming fire taking vengeance on
them that know not God, and that obey
not the gospel of our Lord Jesus Christ.

The Old Testament contains numerous testimonies of the love and merciful loving-kindness of God. And the most striking and fearsome warnings and prophecies of judgment to come are found in the New Testament.

Our text for the day is an example, with its revelation of the coming eternal separation from God of all who reject Christ and His saving gospel. The Lord Jesus Christ Himself uttered more warnings of future hell than anyone else recorded in either Testament. Jude spoke of ungodly men "to whom is reserved the blackness of darkness for ever."

And, of course, the very last book of the New Testament, written by John, the disciple who stressed God's love more than any other writer, focuses in detail on the coming period of God's judgment on a rebellious world. "Whosoever was not found written in the book of life was cast into the lake of fire."

God's grace and full forgiveness are free to all who receive Christ, but certain judgment will come to all who refuse.

Scripture:

2 Thessalonians 1:8-9; Jude 13; Revelation 20:15

Unsearchable and Unspeakable

O the depth of the riches both of the wisdom
and knowledge of God! how unsearchable are
his judgments, and his ways past finding out!

God's majesty and purposes are immeasurably far beyond human words and understanding—unspeakable and unsearchable. He "doeth great things and unsearchable; marvelous things without number." His resources are also beyond anything we can imagine. The apostle Paul spoke about "the unsearchable riches of Christ," and he once had the unique experience of being caught up somehow into the very paradise of God, where he "heard unspeakable words, which it is not lawful for a man to utter."

We can have a good measure of peace and joy right now in Christ, but there is much more yet to learn. In the new earth someday we shall really be able to "rejoice with joy unspeakable and full of glory."

God's great gift of salvation and eternal life we comprehend only faintly now, but we know it is indeed a gift of love and grace and peace and joy! Although we cannot begin to describe it now, we can simply say in gratitude, "Thanks be unto God for his unspeakable gift."

Scripture:
Romans 11:33; Job 5:9; Ephesians 3:8; 2:7;
2 Corinthians 12:4; 9:15; 1 Peter 1:8

Unanswered Prayer

*The eyes of the Lord are over the righteous, and
his ears are open unto their prayers: but the
face of the Lord is against them that do evil.*

Scripture reveals many conditions for answered prayer. For example, Jesus said, "If ye shall ask any thing in my name, I will do it." But in the same upper-room discourse, He also said, "If ye abide in me, and my words abide in you, ye shall ask what ye will, and it shall be done unto you." This is a very significant condition attached to what might have seemed an unconditional promise.

Overt sin in one's life will certainly hinder our prayers. So will selfish praying: "Ye ask, and receive not, because ye ask amiss, that ye may consume it upon your lusts." And so will unbelief: "When ye pray, believe that ye receive them, and ye shall have them." Finally, there is the question of timing. "Men ought always to pray, and not to faint."

Still, we can be sure that the believing prayer of a man righteous before God surely will be answered in God's time and way.

Scripture:
1 Peter 3:7,12; John 14:14; 15:7; James 4:3;
Mark 11:24; Luke 18:1

A Divine Controversy

Hear ye, O mountains, the LORD's controversy,
and ye strong foundations of the earth:
for the LORD hath a controversy with his
people, and he will plead with Israel.

Controversy is uncomfortable, especially when we are at odds with the Lord. Certainly the Jewish nation needed Micah's warning: "O my people, what have I done unto thee? and wherein have I wearied thee? testify against me." The prophet Hosea similarly challenged the people about this divine controversy. "Hear the word of the LORD, ye children of Israel: for the LORD hath a controversy with the inhabitants of the land, because there is no truth, nor mercy, nor knowledge of God in the land."

The religious activity of the people in those days had become mere rote rituals without any emotional relationship. The prophet asked them, "Will the Lord be pleased with thousands of rams, or with ten thousands of rivers of oil?"

God's desire is for our lives to be in conformity to His will, not for us to give Him a formulaic, token religious devotion. "He hath showed thee, O man, what is good; and what doth the LORD require of thee, but to do justly, and to love mercy, and to walk humbly with thy God?"

Scripture:

Micah 6:2-8; Hosea 4:1

The Great Divider

Suppose ye that I am come to give peace on earth? I tell you, Nay; but rather division.

God is the great divider. At creation, He "divided the light from the darkness" and "the waters which were under the firmament from the waters which were above."

When God first created man, they walked together in sweet fellowship, but then sin came in and made a great division between man and God. Nevertheless, "when we were enemies, we were reconciled to God by the death of his Son."

Jesus Christ divides all history into "before Christ" (BC) or "in the year of our Lord" (AD), and into the old covenant or the new covenant.

Most of all, He divides humanity. "There was a division among the people because of him." These divisions because of Him can cut very deep. "The father shall be divided against the son, and the son against the father; the mother against the daughter, and the daughter against the mother."

Finally, when He comes to judge all nations, "he shall separate them one from another, as a shepherd divideth his sheep from the goats...and these shall go away into everlasting punishment: but the righteous into life eternal."

Scripture:
Luke 12:51; Genesis 1:4,7; Romans 5:10; John 7:43;
Luke 12:53; Matthew 25:32,46

A House in the Land of Shinar

*He said unto me, To build it an
house in the land of Shinar.*

This prophecy of the latter days shows a woman named
"wickedness" being translated rapidly in a great measuring
basket—symbolizing commerce and finance "through all the
earth"—to a base being built for it in the ancient land of Shinar (same as Sumeria). This was also the land of Nimrod, the
leader of the post-Flood rebellion against God at Babel. "He
began to be a mighty one in the earth…And the beginning of
his kingdom was Babel…in the land of Shinar."

From this first Babylon in the land of Shinar, the dispersed
followers of Nimrod carried their anti-God, materialistic religion into every land through every age. Its current form is
mainly a pantheistic evolutionary humanism promoting a
"new world order," featuring a world government and (supposedly) universal prosperity without God.

In Revelation, she is called "Mystery, Babylon the Great,
the Mother of Harlots and Abominations of the Earth." She
sits upon "peoples, and multitudes, and nations, and tongues."
This monstrous system is evidently once again to have a house
built for it in the land of Shinar.

Scripture:
Zechariah 5:6-11; Genesis 10:8,10; Revelation 17:5,15

A Truly New Thing

The LORD hath created a new thing in the earth.

Only God can truly create, so a really new thing would have to be produced directly by the Lord Himself. Of course, God completed His original work of creating all things long ago, including a marvelous mechanism for human reproduction. Because of man's sin, He very soon had to begin a work of reconciliation, and this included a primeval promise that "the seed of the woman" would come someday to accomplish this great work.

Isaiah prophesied of this miracle many years later: "A virgin shall conceive, and bear a son," and that Son would be "the mighty God," who would establish His kingdom "with justice from henceforth even for ever."

Jeremiah wrote of this same great promise: God would create, by His mighty power, a new thing, a perfect human body, without inherited sin or physical blemish, and with no contribution from either male or female, in the womb of a specially called virgin. She would compass that "holy thing" with warmth and love as it grew in her womb.

Then, in the fullness of time, "God sent forth his Son, made of a woman" to "save his people from their sins."

Scripture:
Jeremiah 31:22; Genesis 3:15; Isaiah 7:14; 9:6-7;
Galatians 4:4; Matthew 1:21

Christian Adornment

…as a bridegroom decketh himself with ornaments,
and as a bride adorneth herself with her jewels.

The worldly person may dress in costly garments and ornate jewelry, but if these merely attempt to beautify an unregenerate life, they are no better than hastily sown fig-leaf aprons or filthy rags.

Note the admonition of Paul in the New Testament. "I will therefore…that women adorn themselves in modest apparel, with shame-facedness and sobriety; not with broided hair, or gold, or pearls, or costly array." Similarly, to Christian wives, Peter says, "Whose adorning let it not be that outward adorning of plaiting the hair, and of wearing of gold, or of putting on of apparel; but let it be the hidden man of the heart, in that which is not corruptible, even the ornament of a meek and quiet spirit, which is in the sight of God of great price." A Christian should also be clothed in "the whole armor of God." Both by modest clothing and by a Spirit-controlled life, we thus ought to "adorn the doctrine of God our Savior in all things."

Scripture:
Isaiah 61:10; 64:6; Genesis 3:7,21; 1 Timothy 2:8-10;
1 Peter 3:3-4; Titus 2:10; Ephesians 6:11,14-17

Christian Submission

*He went down with them, and came to
Nazareth, and was subject unto them: but his
mother kept all these sayings in her heart.*

Christians are frequently exhorted to submit themselves to
others. Wives, for example, are told, "Submit yourselves
unto your own husbands, as unto the Lord." Similarly, Paul
told Titus to urge Christian slaves "to be obedient [same Greek
word] unto their own masters."

Christians are told to "obey them that have the rule over
you, and submit yourselves: for they watch for your souls, as
they that must give account." We are also commanded to be
in submission to government officials whether they are Christian or not. "Submit yourselves to every ordinance of man
for the Lord's sake," says the apostle Peter. Similarly Paul said,
"Let every soul be subject [same Greek word again] unto the
higher powers."

Our willingness to yield our own ways to others must go
even further than this. "All of you be subject one to another,
and be clothed with humility."

Finally, we need to remember that "God resisteth the
proud, but giveth grace unto the humble. Submit yourselves
therefore to God."

Scripture:
Luke 2:51; Ephesians 5:21-22; Titus 2:9; Hebrews 13:17;
1 Peter 2:13; 5:5; Romans 13:1; James 4:6-7

The Death of Pride

*Then said Jesus unto his disciples, If any man
will come after me, let him deny himself,
and take up his cross, and follow me.*

Where Christ speaks about the cross, the context always includes the believer's daily dying to one's self. "He that findeth his life shall lose it: and he that loseth his life for my sake shall find it."

In the first discourse on the cross in Matthew 10, Jesus says, "He that loveth father or mother more than me is not worthy of me…And he that taketh not his cross, and followeth after me, is not worthy of me."

"Whosoever therefore shall be ashamed of me and of my words in this adulterous and sinful generation; of him also shall the Son of man be ashamed, when he cometh in the glory of his Father with the holy angels."

John's Gospel is the only one that does not specifically mention taking up our cross daily; however, he does mention those whose pride was so great they were not willing to do so. "They loved the praise of men more than the praise of God."

Scripture:

Matthew 16:24; 10:37-39; Mark 8:38; John 12:42-43

Stubbornness

Rebellion is as the sin of witchcraft, and
stubbornness is as iniquity and idolatry.

Soon after God delivered the Israelites from Egypt, they
made a golden calf, entering into idolatrous worship. Were
it not for Moses' intercession, they would have been destroyed.
He prayed, "Remember thy servants, Abraham, Isaac, and
Jacob; look not unto the stubbornness of this people." Many
years later, the psalmist Asaph prayed that the nation "might
not be as their fathers, a stubborn and rebellious generation."

King Saul stubbornly refused to destroy all the Amalekites.
He kept alive King Agag and the best of the animals. Samuel described this disobedience as rebellion and stubbornness,
comparing it to the sins of witchcraft and idolatry.

The law warns Jewish sons about stubbornness. "Then
shall his father and his mother lay hold on him, and bring
him out unto the elders of his city…and they shall say…This
our son is stubborn and rebellious, he will not obey our voice…
And all the men of his city shall stone him with stones."

And Proverbs gives a warning concerning a fallen woman.
She is described as being "loud and stubborn; her feet abide
not in her house."

Scripture:
1 Samuel 15:23; Deuteronomy 9:27; 21:18-21;
Psalm 78:8; Proverbs 7:11

Multigenerational Wisdom

I was my father's son, tender and only
beloved in the sight of my mother.

Solomon credits his parents for instructing him in the way of wisdom. The famous insights into a virtuous woman are specifically attributed to his mother, Bathsheba: "The words of king Lemuel, the prophecy that his mother taught him."

But this wisdom can be traced back even earlier in this family. For we know that the grandfather of Bathsheba was the wise advisor Ahithophel. "And the counsel of Ahithophel, which he counseled in those days, was as if a man had enquired at the oracle of God."

God places a high premium on parents who will convey the wisdom of God's revelation to subsequent generations. We read one of the reasons Abraham was given special consideration: "He will command his children and his household after him, and they shall keep the way of the LORD, to do justice and judgment."

In the New Testament Paul noted that his "son in the faith" was the recipient of such a godly inheritance: "first in thy grandmother Lois, and thy mother Eunice; and I am persuaded that in thee also."

Scripture:
Proverbs 4:1,3-4; 31:1; 2 Samuel 16:23; Genesis 18:19;
2 Timothy 1:5; Deuteronomy 6:6-7

Mother Birds and Their Young

If a bird's nest chance to be before thee
in the way in any tree, or on the ground,
whether they be young ones, or eggs…

The blessing of prolonged days previously came with the commandment to honor your father and mother, but it is repeated in our text with respect to birds. The Lord, who instills in animals concern for their young, wants His people to respect that relationship.

There is a related command: "When a bullock, or a sheep, or a goat, is brought forth, then it shall be seven days under the dam…And whether it be cow or ewe, ye shall not kill it and her young both in one day." Why this concern for animals and their young? The Lord Jesus, Maker of all, said that His Father knows when a sparrow falls to the ground.

Some Christians, professing to believe the Bible, kowtow to academics who speak of animals becoming extinct supposedly millions of years before Adam sinned, the inference being that God must be cruel. The world became corrupt, however, through Adam and Eve; extinctions followed. The faith statement that the world is millions or billions of years old clashes with the words of Jesus.

Scripture:
Deuteronomy 22:6-7; Leviticus 22:27-28; Matthew 10:29

The Empowering Touch of God

The LORD put forth his hand, and touched
my mouth. And the LORD said unto me,
Behold, I have put my words in thy mouth.

I t is fascinating to note the various parts of the human body that God is said to have touched. For example, when God touched Jeremiah's mouth, the prophet was enabled to speak divinely inspired words to his people.

Similarly, when Christ met two blind men who believed in His power, "touched he their eyes…And their eyes were opened," thereby energizing them to "spread abroad his fame in all that country." Likewise, He gave a deaf and dumb man the ability to hear and speak with the result that all those who observed the miracle "published it" widely, saying, "He hath done all things well."

In one instance, the touch of God increased spiritual power: "He touched the hollow of his thigh; and the hollow of Jacob's thigh was out of joint…And he said…as a prince hast thou power with God and with men."

The Lord need not physically touch our mouth or eyes or ears or hand today, but He can and does touch our hearts.

Scripture:
Jeremiah 1:9; Matthew 9:29-31; 8:14-15; Mark 7:33-37;
Genesis 32:25,28

The Indwelling Christ

They glorified God in me.

"Christ liveth in me," said the apostle Paul, and because that was true experientially as well as doctrinally, he could invite people to see Christ and hear Christ and follow Christ by seeing and hearing and following him. He also commanded, "Those things, which ye have both learned, and received, and heard, and seen in me, do: and the God of peace shall be with you."

The Lord could say to His disciples, "He that hath seen me hath seen the Father," and no one thinks it inappropriate, because He fully manifested the heavenly Father in word and deed.

This was not boasting, for Paul acknowledged that "in me (that is, in my flesh,) dwelleth no good thing." Still, he was bold to exhort, "Be ye followers of me, even as I also am of Christ."

The same Spirit of Christ who dwelled in Paul also indwells all true Christians, for "if any man have not the Spirit of Christ, he is none of his." We should be able to say with Paul, in practice as well as theory, "Christ liveth in me."

Scripture:
Galatians 1:24; 2:20; Philippians 4:9; John 14:9;
Romans 7:18; 8:9; 1 Corinthians 11:1

Rest for the People of God

*There remaineth therefore a rest
to the people of God.*

The Lord knew His people would need rest and so ordained a weekly day of rest. In fact, the only reason He took six days to do the work of creation was to set the pattern for man's six-day workweek.

The Scriptures command us to be always "redeeming the time, because the days are evil," so concerned Christians often have difficulty finding time for needed rest, even on the Sabbath days, let alone an annual vacation.

The Greek word translated "rest" is actually the special word for "Sabbath rest," used only this one time in the New Testament, evidently indicating that the weekly rest day is still a divine principle, and we violate it to our detriment. It also refers, in context, to the rest we find in Christ, "for he that is entered into his rest, he also hath ceased from his own works, as God did from his."

For now, however, even when it is hard to find time for physical rest, we find rest for our souls in Christ.

Scripture:

Hebrews 4:9-10; Exodus 20:8-11; Ephesians 5:16

Neighbor Relations

Be not a witness against thy
neighbor without cause.

King Ahab wanted the vineyard of his neighbor, Naboth. But Naboth refused, so Ahab's wife Jezebel devised a plot to steal it. Her plan was to proclaim a fast…"and set two men, sons of Belial, before him [Naboth], to bear witness against him, saying, Thou didst blaspheme God and the king. And then carry him out, and stone him, that he may die." Lying about Naboth signed his death warrant.

"One witness shall not rise up against a man for any iniquity, or for any sin, in any sin that he sinneth: at the mouth of two witnesses, or at the mouth of three witnesses, shall the matter be established." One can understand the importance of the ninth commandment: "Thou shalt not bear false witness against thy neighbor."

A lawyer once asked Jesus, "Who is my neighbor?" Jesus' answer is the well-known story of the good Samaritan. Then He asked the question, "Which now of these three, thinkest thou, was neighbor unto him that fell among the thieves?" The lawyer answered that the neighbor was the one who showed mercy—the Good Samaritan.

Scripture:
Proverbs 24:28-29; 1 Kings 21:10,13; Deuteronomy 19:15;
Exodus 20:16; Luke 10:29,36-37

The Poetry of God

We are his workmanship, created in Christ
Jesus unto good works, which God hath before
ordained that we should walk in them.

The word "poem" is derived from the Greek word *poiema*. Used only twice in the New Testament, it refers to great works of God Himself. Thus, God is the divine poet who has created two great masterpieces—artistic creations of marvelous intricacy and surpassing beauty.

The first is the entire physical universe: "For the invisible things of him from the creation of the world are clearly seen, being understood by the things that are made, even his eternal power and Godhead; so that they are without excuse." In this key verse, *poiema* is translated "things that are made."

Yet an even more amazing poem is the work of transforming redemption accomplished in a lost soul saved by grace through faith, for then we ourselves become His poem! This also is a great creative masterpiece, for "we are his workmanship [same word, Greek *poiema*], created in Christ Jesus unto good works."

A life once dead in sin, now born again and walking in good works—this is God's greatest poetic masterpiece of all!

Scripture:
Ephesians 2:10; Romans 1:20

In a Moment of Time

*The devil, taking him up into an high
mountain, showed unto him all the kingdoms
of the world in a moment of time.*

It is interesting that there are just three "moments" mentioned in the New Testament and that there are three different Greek words so translated, each used one time only in the Bible.

First of all, Satan tempted Jesus by giving Him a vision of the whole world, offering it to Him immediately without His having to endure the cross—if He would rule it for the devil. Here the Greek word for "moment" is *stigme*, meaning a "point," like a period after a sentence.

One day, Jesus will return to reclaim the world from Satan. At that great day, "we shall all be changed, in a moment, in the twinkling of an eye." In this passage, the unique word is *atomos*, meaning an indivisible particle.

Right now, however, our bodies are weak and easily beset with pain and sickness. Nevertheless, we are assured that "our light affliction, which is but for a moment, worketh for us a far more exceeding and eternal weight of glory." The word here is *parautika*, referring specifically to the present moment.

Scripture:
Luke 4:5; 1 Corinthians 15:51-52; 2 Corinthians 4:17

Mindful of the Words

*Be mindful of the words which were
spoken before by the holy prophets.*

There has long been a tendency for certain Bible teachers to water down the doctrine of verbal inspiration by arguing that it is the thoughts of Scripture that count, not the precise words. They forget that the transmission of specific thoughts requires precise words. Ambiguous language is bound to produce fuzzy thinking and uncertain response.

John warned of the grave danger incurred by anyone who would either "add to" or "take away from," not just the ideas, but "the words of the prophecy of this book."

Jesus frequently quoted passages from the Old Testament, sometimes basing His entire thrust on a single word. He stressed that "the scripture cannot be broken," referring to the actual words written by Moses and the prophets.

Near the end of His earthly ministry, He made a startling promise: "Heaven and earth shall pass away: but my words shall not pass away." Thus the actual words of the Bible have come ultimately from God, and we do well to learn them and make them a part of our lives.

Scripture:

2 Peter 3:2; Revelation 22:18-19; John 10:35; Mark 13:31

The Stars Forever

*They that be wise shall shine as the brightness
of the firmament; and they that turn many to
righteousness as the stars for ever and ever.*

The setting of this beautiful verse is after the resurrection of the saved to everlasting life, and the unsaved to eternal shame. Its glorious promise to those who are "wise" and who "turn many to righteousness" through Jesus Christ is that they will shine like stars forever.

Evolutionary astronomers believe that stars evolve through a long cycle of stellar life and death, but God revealed that He has created this physical universe to last forever.

Because of sin "the whole creation groaneth...until now," and the heavens "shall wax old as doth a garment...and they shall be changed." In fact, the earth and its atmospheric heaven (not the sidereal heaven) one day will "pass away," and then will be transformed by God into "new heavens and a new earth" which will never pass away.

The stars are innumerable, each one unique, each one with a divine purpose, and they will shine forever. We can never reach them in this life, but in our glorified bodies, we shall have endless time to explore the infinite heavens.

Scripture:
Daniel 12:3; Romans 8:22; Hebrews 1:11-12;
Matthew 24:35; 2 Peter 3:13

The Stars Also

God made two great lights; the greater
light to rule the day, and the lesser light to
rule the night: he made the stars also.

Earth is the center of God's interest in the universe. This is where He created man and woman in His own image and where He will reign over His creation in the ages to come.

The primary purpose of the stars, as well as the sun and moon, was "to divide the day from the night; and…to be for signs, and for seasons, and for days, and years: and…to give light upon the earth." They could not fulfill these functions, of course, if their light could not be seen on the earth, so we can be sure that these heavenly bodies and their light rays were created—like Adam and Eve—"full-grown," in a state of functioning maturity.

All that can be known scientifically about the stars must be determined from their light intensity and spectra. Although the stars all look alike (even through a telescope, they all appear as mere points of light), these calculations have shown that each one is unique, as revealed long ago in Scripture: "One star differeth from another star in glory."

Scripture:
Genesis 1:14-16; 1 Corinthians 15:41

The Two Hosts of Heaven

I saw the LORD sitting upon his throne,
and all the host of heaven standing on
his right hand and on his left.

Scripture confirms that there really is a great host of angels at God's throne in heaven. These are mighty angels, and they go forth at God's command, especially in connection with their primary function as "ministering spirits, sent forth to minister for them who shall be heirs of salvation."

In addition to the angels, there is another "host of heaven"—the stars, which "cannot be numbered." Like the stars, the angels also are said to be "innumerable." Both "hosts" are mentioned in Nehemiah 9:6. Angels are often associated with stars in the Bible and are even likened to stars on a number of occasions.

However, a third of the angels "kept not their first estate." It is this particular "host of heaven" which all devotees of false religions, ancient and modern, have really worshipped when they reject the true God of creation and put their faith in some aspect of the cosmos itself. The faithful and obedient host of heaven worships God alone, and so should we.

Scripture:
2 Chronicles 18:18; Psalm 103:20-21; Jeremiah 33:22;
Hebrews 1:14; 12:22

The Complex Cosmos

He hath made the earth by his power, he hath
established the world by his wisdom, and hath
stretched out the heavens by his discretion.

This verse gives a fascinating insight into God's primeval creation of the universe. "Earth" refers to the geosphere, or the inorganic components of the globe; the "world" is its biosphere, especially the plant life; and the "heavens" are the atmosphere and astrosphere.

God's amazing "power" surpasses even the tremendous energy or force required to organize the complex systems and physicochemical processes governing the earth. The "wisdom" of God speaks of the skillful planning by which He set up the plant biosphere and the hydrologic systems to maintain it. His "discretion" is the infinite intelligence necessary to spread out the infinite cosmos filled with innumerable stars and clusters of stars.

The two preceding verses say it well. "But the LORD is the true God, he is the living God, and an everlasting king… The gods that have not made the heavens and the earth, even they shall perish from the earth, and from under these heavens." We do well, therefore, to trust Him in all things. "I am the LORD," says He, "the God of all flesh: is there anything too hard for me?"

Scripture:

Jeremiah 10:10-12; 32:27

Prosperity Versus Contentment

Godliness with contentment is great gain.

Contentment is a rare commodity. There is a widespread error among born-again Christians that material prosperity is a token of spirituality and of divine approval on an affluent lifestyle.

However, such affluence should be regarded as a testing, for Jesus said, "Unto whomsoever much is given, of him shall be much required." Paul was perhaps the most faithful and fruitful Christian who ever lived, yet he died penniless in a Roman dungeon. His own testimony concerning material possessions and standards of living was this: "I have learned, in whatsoever state I am, therewith to be content. I know both how to be abased, and I know how to abound: every where and in all things I am instructed both to be full and to be hungry, both to abound and to suffer need."

In the context of today's key verse, the apostle Paul has actually been warning young Pastor Timothy against the influence of those who suppose, among other things, that "gain is godliness" and who think that their material prosperity is proof of their spiritual prosperity. "From such" says Paul, "withdraw thyself."

Scripture:
1 Timothy 6:5-6; Luke 12:48; Philippians 4:11-12

Wondrous Things in the Word

Open thou mine eyes, that I may behold
wondrous things out of thy law.

The word "law" (Hebrew, *torah*), as used in the Psalms, actually refers to all the revealed Scriptures. And we can indeed behold wondrous things in the Word if we have eyes to see and hearts to believe by the grace of God.

The adjective "wondrous" is often used to describe God's mighty miracles in Egypt and elsewhere. This would indicate that there are many evidences of divine origin that can be gleaned from the Scriptures.

Psalm 119 itself illustrates this truth. It has 22 stanzas (keyed to the 22 letters of the Hebrew alphabet), each with 8 verses (the number 8 representing new life). The 176 verses (8 times 22)—the most in any chapter in the Bible—have 176 references to the Holy Scriptures.

The great theme of the psalm is, therefore, the wonder and power of the life-giving, written Word of God. Just as the Lord Jesus was raised from the dead on the "eighth day," and as there are eight other instances of the dead being restored to life in the Bible, there are eight different Hebrew words used for the Scriptures in the psalm.

Scripture:
Psalm 119:18; 2 Timothy 3:15

Where Is Wisdom?

Where shall wisdom be found? and
where is the place of understanding?

Men have been searching for this most valuable of all treasures since time began. Eve first fell into sin as she was led by Satan to believe that the forbidden fruit would make her wise. Even before Abram left Ur of the Chaldees, the patriarch Job was asking this ancient question of his three critical friends, but they could not answer.

Job notes that valuable metals can be dug from the rocks of the earth, but wisdom cannot be mined by hard searching and labor. It cannot be purchased like a commodity. Neither can it be acquired through college degrees, philosophical meditation, or any variety of human experience or study.

It can only be found in God Himself, for "God understandeth the way thereof, and he knoweth the place thereof." Job understood that the "fear of the LORD, that is wisdom; and to depart from evil is understanding."

True wisdom is to be found in the Lord Jesus, "who of God is made unto us wisdom." In Him alone "are hid all the treasures of wisdom and knowledge."

Scripture:
Job 28:12,23,28; 1 Corinthians 1:30; Colossians 2:3

Ascending Vapors

He causeth the vapors to ascend
from the ends of the earth.

This striking verse is practically identical with Jeremiah 10:13 and Jeremiah 51:16, suggesting the possibility that the prophet Jeremiah may have written the otherwise anonymous Psalm 135. The two Jeremiah passages do preface this statement with the note that there is "a multitude of waters in the heavens" in connection with the processes described in the verse.

In any case, this thrice-mentioned mechanism beautifully summarizes what we now call the hydrologic cycle, and it did so more than 2000 years before the cycle began to be understood by modern scientists. In order to provide rain to water the earth, there must be vapors ascending all over the earth (that is, evaporation from the world's great oceans), winds blowing from God's unseen "treasuries" (actually the global atmospheric circulation), and finally, "lightnings for [or with] the rain" (electrical discharges associated with the condensation and coalescence of the particles of water vapor in the atmosphere).

These repeatedly transport purified waters from the ocean back over the lands to fall as rain and snow, there finally to flow back to the oceans after performing their life-sustaining ministries on the lands. "Unto the place from whence the rivers come, thither they return again."

Scripture:
Psalm 135:7; Ecclesiastes 1:7

Afraid to Understand

They understood not that saying, and
were afraid to ask him.

When the Lord Jesus told His disciples about His coming death and resurrection, He could hardly have spoken more plainly, yet they "understood not." Not willing to believe that He meant what He said (with all its uncomfortable implications for their own futures), they were "afraid to ask him" what He meant, lest He confirm that His words should be taken literally.

This was not the only time. Again and again, He told them He would be crucified and then rise again, but they could not (or would not) understand. On one such occasion, Peter even rebuked Him: "Lord: this shall not be unto thee," but the Lord answered, "Get thee behind me, Satan." A refusal to take God's Word literally, at least in this case, was said by Christ to be inspired by Satan.

Fearful reluctance to take God's Word literally is still a great problem among some "Bible-believers." Whenever such a stand might become costly, many Christians eagerly accept nonliteral ways of interpreting Scripture to fit their own preferences. This approach, of course, is especially widespread in modern accommodations of the creation and Flood accounts in Genesis to the philosophies of modern evolutionary humanism.

Scripture:
Mark 9:31-32; Matthew 16:22-23

The Witness of Creation

Seek him that maketh the seven
stars… The LORD is his name.

This striking exhortation is inserted in the midst of a prophetic rebuke by God of His people Israel. They were rapidly drifting into pagan idolatry, and Amos was trying to call them back.

His exhortation, given almost 2800 years ago, is more needed today than ever before. Modern pagan scientists have developed elaborate but absurdly impossible theories about the chance origin of the universe from nothing and the evolution of stars, planets, and people from primordial hydrogen. But the mighty cosmos and its galaxies of stars were made by an omniscient, omnipotent Creator, who had a glorious purpose for it all.

Similarly, the global evidences that waters once covered all the earth's mountains cannot possibly be explained by slow processes acting over eons of time. God the Creator had to call massive volumes of water forth from their original reservoirs and pour them out on the earth in His judgment on a rebellious world.

All of these witness to creation and judgment by an all-powerful God.

Scripture:

Amos 5:8

Created and Made

*These are the generations of the heavens and of
the earth when they were created, in the day that
the LORD God made the earth and the heavens.*

There are two accounts of creation in Genesis, with the
above text marking the dividing point. In the first, the
name used for the Creator is "God" (Hebrew, *Elohim*), and
its termination is the summarizing signature: "These are the
generations (Hebrew, *toledoth*) of the heavens and of the earth
when they were created."

The second account normally uses the name "LORD God"
(*Jehovah Elohim*) in chapters 2 and 3 (except where the serpent and Eve used *Elohim* in their conversation) and then
simply "LORD" (Hebrew, *Jehovah*) in chapter 4. This second
creation account ends with Adam's signature: "This is the book
of the generations [*toledoth*] of Adam."

Critics claim that the two accounts are contradictory.
Actually they are complementary, the second merely giving
more details of the events of the fifth and sixth days of creation week. The Lord Jesus quoted both accounts at the same
time in the same context.

The heavens and the earth were both "created" and "made."

Scripture:
Genesis 1:1–5:1; Matthew 19:4-6

Creation and United Prayer

They lifted up their voice to God with
one accord, and said, Lord, thou art
God, which hast made heaven, and earth,
and the sea, and all that in them is.

When Christians can unite in acknowledging God as true omnipotent Creator (as did the early disciples), they can pray in confidence regardless of all the "threatenings" of those who are "gathered together against the Lord, and against his Christ." The God who called the infinite cosmos into existence with all its creatures can easily handle those who seek to thwart His will.

But Christians do not speak with one accord today, even on this most basic of all truths—the fact of creation. Instead, many choose to dissemble and equivocate and compromise, inventing such self-contradictory concepts as theistic evolution, progressive creation, process creation, and the like. Loving "the praise of men more than the praise of God," they seek academic approval rather than biblical authority and scientific factuality.

There can be no real Christian unity until there is one accord on the foundation of Christian unity.

Scripture:
Acts 4:24-33; John 12:43

Watch and Pray

We made our prayer unto our God, and
set a watch against them day and night.

Prayer is a powerful weapon, but the wall builders in Jerusalem also were careful to set a watch against their enemies "with their swords, their spears, and their bows." They were ready to fight if necessary, but at the same time they were confident: "Our God shall fight for us."

God expects us to make appropriate use of whatever physical means are available for a needed ministry. The Lord rebuked those who asked Him to perform a miracle merely to test Him or to see something curious. "Except ye see signs and wonders, ye will not believe." Neither does He condone prayer in lieu of work, for "faith, if it hath not works, is dead, being alone."

But as prayer without working is dead, so watching and working without prayer are futile. "Except the LORD build the house, they labor in vain that build it: except the LORD keep the city, the watchman waketh but in vain."

The biblical principle is not only to watch or only to pray. Both are essential. "Watch and pray," said Jesus, "that ye enter not into temptation."

Scripture:
Nehemiah 4:9-20; John 4:48; James 2:17;
Psalm 127:1; Matthew 26:41

Prayer for All

I exhort therefore, that, first of all,
supplications, prayers, intercessions, and
giving of thanks, be made for all men.

Intercession is a great gift that any Christian can give, even if he is penniless or bedridden. There are none so poor as to be unable to afford such a gift, and even the wealthiest can give no finer gift.

First, we are to pray for all fellow Christians, "praying always with all prayer and supplication in the Spirit, and watching thereunto with all perseverance and supplication for all saints." We should also pray for the lost. Jesus commanded, "The harvest truly is great, but the laborers are few: pray ye therefore the Lord of the harvest, that he would send forth laborers into his harvest."

There is a special command to pray for sick disciples. "Pray one for another, that ye may be healed." We are even told to pray for our enemies. "Bless them that curse you, and pray for them which despitefully use you."

In short, we should offer up supplications, prayers, intercessions, and thanksgiving for all men everywhere, "for this is the will of God in Christ Jesus concerning you."

Scripture:
1 Timothy 2:1; Ephesians 6:18; Luke 10:2; 6:28;
James 5:16; 1 Thessalonians 5:18

Let Them Pray

Is any among you afflicted? let him pray.

Many suffering Christians have tried in all sincerity to follow the instructions given here yet have not been healed. This may be because the promise has a specific application rather than a general one.

First, the word "afflicted" means "troubled," referring especially to persecution or deprivation. For such a person, the admonition is, "Let him pray." Assuming that he is right with God and praying in His will, he can expect either the needed relief or the needed grace.

Second, "Is any sick?" The context shows that this particular sickness has come specifically "if he have committed sins." The remedy is for such a person to call for the church elders (not the reverse) and to "let them pray" in faith (after he has first openly confessed and repented of his sins), anointing him with oil. Then the promise is that, if the elders themselves have faith and are right with God, the Lord will forgive his sins and raise him up.

There are other reasons for illness besides sin without repentance, but this is a wonderful promise of both spiritual and physical healing when sin is the problem.

Scripture:

James 5:13-15

Pray Without Ceasing

Praying always with all prayer and
supplication in the Spirit.

Paul's command to "pray without ceasing" is obviously to be understood metaphorically (after all, we do have to sleep and work as well as pray), but it is also to be taken seriously.

Even during waking hours, of course, the attitude of unceasing general prayer is not meant to supersede special periods of concentrated prayer. Jesus taught about prayer in the Sermon on the Mount: "When thou prayest, enter into thy closet, and when thou hast shut thy door, pray to thy Father which is in secret."

Christ Himself has set an example: "In the morning, rising up a great while before day, he went out, and departed into a solitary place, and there prayed."

The words of our text imply not a continual verbalized prayer, but a continual attitude of prayer and watchfulness, whereby it becomes easy and natural to breathe a short (but sincere) prayer "in the Spirit" whenever a need appears. Thus, whether at work or at rest, we can—as Paul exhorts—"continue in prayer, and watch in the same with thanksgiving."

Scripture:
Ephesians 6:18; 1 Thessalonians 5:17; Matthew 6:6;
Mark 1:35; Colossians 4:2

Pray Anyhow

As for me, God forbid that I should sin
against the LORD in ceasing to pray for you.

Israel wanted a king and pressed the prophet and judge Samuel to get one for them. Both Samuel and the Lord Himself were displeased with the Israelites' demand, but eventually, according to God's direction, Samuel anointed Saul to be their king.

Samuel's great heart, both for the Lord and for His people, is revealed in the promise of our text. He had led Israel successfully and justly his whole life. He was hurt and disappointed by their request; nevertheless, he would still pray for them and teach them. This is a great example for Christian leaders or workers today who, through no fault of their own, have been replaced by someone else.

Intercessory prayer is not easy, especially if our prayers are not appreciated by those we pray for. Nevertheless, this prayer ministry especially pleases the Lord, and *that* is more important than human gratitude.

"I exhort therefore" said Paul, "that, first of all, supplications, prayers, intercessions, and giving of thanks, be made for all men; for kings, and for all that are in authority."

Scripture:
1 Samuel 12:23; 1 Timothy 2:1-2

268

When Not to Pray

The LORD said unto Joshua, Get thee up;
wherefore liest thou thus upon thy face?

After the mighty victory at Jericho, it was abundantly obvious that God was fighting for His people as they entered the land of Canaan. God had promised Joshua, "There shall not any man be able to stand before thee all the days of thy life," so nothing could stop them now.

Normally, prayer is a good thing, especially in times of great need, such as this. Yet God rebuked Joshua for praying at Ai. There is a time to pray and a time *not* to pray.

Israel's lack of success at Ai could only have resulted from their disobedience. Joshua, as leader, should have realized this and should have proceeded to punish those responsible. Instead, he was groveling and complaining with his face on the ground.

As soon as Joshua purged the guilty ones from the company, which he should have done in the first place, God gave Israel a great victory over those who had once defeated them.

We have no right to pray if we are harboring known sin. Even if there is no known sin, unanswered prayer is at least a cause for careful self-examination.

Scripture:
Joshua 1:5,8; 7:6-10; 8:34

How to Pray

Hitherto have ye asked nothing in my name: ask,
and ye shall receive, that your joy may be full.

"In my name" implies representing Christ and what He stands for so that our prayer could truly be His prayer as well. For example, our prayer must be in His will. "If we ask any thing according to his will…we know that we have the petitions that we desired of him." We need to recognize that God's great purpose in creation is of higher priority than our own personal desires, so this should be of first order in our prayers.

Jesus taught us, "When ye pray, say, Our Father…Thy kingdom come. Thy will be done, as in heaven, so in earth." We can also pray for our own needs, of course, especially for God to "deliver us from evil," the closing request in Jesus' model prayer.

It is good to seek God's wisdom in all our decisions and undertakings so we can be confident we are indeed in His will, but our request for such guidance must be sincere and in willingness to act on His answer. "If any of you lack wisdom, let him ask of God…But let him ask in faith."

Scripture:

John 16:23-24; 1 John 5:14-15; Luke 11:2,4; James 1:5-6

Two Ways

Enter ye in at the strait gate: for wide is the gate,
and broad is the way, that leadeth to destruction.

Multitudes are traveling the broad way to destruction. God Himself, through Jesus Christ, said that few ever find the way to eternal life. That narrow way to life is only through Christ, who said, "I am the way, the truth, and the life: no man cometh unto the Father, but by me."

The words translated "way" in the Old and New Testaments refer to a road or journey. Figuratively, "way" is often used for a lifestyle. The Bible makes it plain, again and again, that there are two ways and two destinies. "The Lord knoweth the way of the righteous: but the way of the ungodly shall perish."

The first "way" mentioned in Scripture is "the way of the tree of life," guarded by mighty cherubim and a flaming sword after Adam and Eve rejected the authority of their Creator. The second "way" mentioned is when "all flesh had corrupted his way upon the earth," and God had to decree "the end of all flesh."

Scripture:

Matthew 7:13-14; John 14:6; Psalm 1:6; Genesis 3:24; 6:12-13

Watchful Sobriety

*Be sober, be vigilant; because your adversary
the devil, as a roaring lion, walketh
about, seeking whom he may devour.*

Several words are used in Scripture to imply spiritual watch-fulness, and each has a slightly different meaning.

"Take ye heed [Greek, *agrupneo*], watch and pray: for ye know not when the time is." The word literally means "be sleepless." It implies a purposeful and active state of awareness.

More commonly used is *gregoreo*. It is a stronger word, meaning to arouse oneself and shake off lethargy, implying activity. "Watch ye, stand fast in the faith," and "continue in prayer, and watch in the same with thanksgiving." "Watch ye, therefore: for ye know not when the master of the house cometh."

A third word is *nepho*, which literally means to abstain from drink that would produce stupor and sleep, and therefore conveys the additional idea of sobriety. By combining the teaching of these three words, we are instructed not only to keep awake but to keep active and to avoid the intoxication of this world's seductive pleasures.

Scripture:

1 Peter 5:8; Mark 13:33,35; 1 Corinthians 16:13;
Colossians 4:2

Our Daily Bread

Give us this day our daily bread.

This very short and very familiar verse contains the only occurrence of the word "daily" in the New Testament and thus emphasizes the fact that we should ask the Lord for our material needs for just one day at a time—not our weekly wages or our annual salary, but our daily bread.

"Therefore take no thought [that is, have no anxiety], saying, what shall we eat? or, What shall we drink?...But seek ye first the kingdom of God, and his righteousness; and all these things shall be added unto you." These words of comfort and assurance by the Lord to believers include the condition that we put God and His kingdom first.

This is also the emphasis in the Lord's model prayer. The prayer begins neither with personal thanksgiving nor with personal requests. Instead, it acknowledges that the most important things are our Creator's purposes for His creation rather than our own material needs. "Thy kingdom come. Thy will be done in earth, as it is in heaven," we are first to pray. Only then should we make our personal requests.

Scripture:
Matthew 6:10-11,31,33

The Truth in Us

…for the truth's sake, which dwelleth in
us, and shall be with us for ever.

The word "truth" occurs more in the Gospel of John than in any other book of the New Testament, and it occurs in the first epistle of John more than in any other book except John's Gospel. It occurs more in both of John's one-chapter epistles than in any other New Testament book save John and 1 John.

God is, indeed, the God of truth, and His written word is "the scripture of truth."

The Lord Jesus Christ is, in fact, the very incarnation of truth. "I am the way, the truth, and the life," He asserted.

Surely truth dwells forever in Christ, for He is the Creator and is thereby the very definition of truth. But how can truth dwell in us and be with us forever? This is certainly not the case with the natural man.

This can be fulfilled only by the Holy Spirit, of course, and this is what Christ has promised. "I will pray the Father, and he shall give you another Comforter, that he may abide with you for ever; even the Spirit of truth."

Scripture:

2 John 2; Daniel 10:21; John 14:6,16-17

Useless Prayers

*He that turneth away his ear from hearing the
law, even his prayer shall be abomination.*

God hates some prayers, strange as that may seem. In fact,
our very prayers can even "become sin." When one delib-
erately "turneth away his ear" from the Word of God and pre-
fers his own way to God's revealed will as found in His Word,
but then attempts to ask God for blessing or direction, his
prayer becomes presumption.

God hates such prayers, and those who pray them should
not be surprised when He does not give them their request.
"The Lord's hand is not shortened, that it cannot save; neither
his ear heavy, that it cannot hear: but your iniquities have separated between you and your God, and your sins have hid his
face from you, that he will not hear."

No Christian is sinless, of course. "If we say that we have
no sin, we deceive ourselves." The obvious remedy is first to
make this request of the Lord: "See if there be any wicked way
in me." Then we must confess and forsake any sin that He
reveals. "If we confess our sins, he is faithful and just to forgive us our sins, and to cleanse us from all unrighteousness."

Scripture:
Proverbs 28:9; Psalm 109:7; 139:4,24;
Isaiah 59:1-2; 1 John 1:8-9

Jesus' Care for His Mother

When Jesus therefore saw his mother…

To the end, the Lord showed His love and concern for His mother—even when He was dying, for He knew that a sword was piercing through her own soul also.

It is uncertain as to why, when Jesus had various brothers and sisters, He had to ask John to take care of His mother. During His earthly ministry, "neither did his brethren believe in him," and it is possible that this had created a problem. If so, at least two of His brothers, James and Jude, later became believers, so perhaps this family division—if such it was—was later resolved.

In any case, at the cross, the Lord asked John to treat Mary as his own mother, and He asked Mary to rely on John as she would her own son. Despite the fact that John's real mother was also there at the cross, he gladly accepted this responsibility.

Mary was evidently at John's home on the morning of the resurrection. When John and Peter realized that Christ had been raised from the dead, they hurried "away again unto their own home," no doubt to tell Mary the glad news. She was also with all the disciples in the upper room as they waited and prayed until the Holy Spirit came to them on the day of Pentecost.

Scripture:
John 19:26-27; Luke 2:35; Matthew 13:55-56; 27:56;
John 7:5; 20:10; 1:14

God with Us

*Adam knew Eve his wife; and she
conceived, and bare Cain, and said, I
have gotten a man from the LORD.*

Here is Eve's testimony concerning the first child born to the human race. To understand it, we need to recall God's first promise: "I will put enmity between thee and the woman, and between thy seed and her seed; [He] shall bruise thy head, and thou shalt bruise his heel."

These words, addressed to Satan, promised that the woman's "seed" would destroy Satan. Thus, that seed would have to be a man, but the only one capable of destroying Satan is God Himself.

More than three millennia later, essentially the same promise was renewed to the "house of David" when the Lord said, "Behold, a virgin shall conceive, and bear a son, and shall call his name Immanuel." This verse reflects the primeval promise that the divine-human Savior, when He came, would be born uniquely as the woman's seed, not of the father's seed like all other men. His very name, Immanuel, means "God with us." He is "the Word…made flesh."

Scripture:
Genesis 4:1; 3:15; Isaiah 7:13-14; Matthew 1:23; John 1:14

Sit Still

*Sit still, my daughter, until thou know how
the matter will fall: for the man will not be in
rest, until he have finished the thing this day.*

This was the instruction Naomi gave to Ruth in hopes that her kinsman, Boaz, would be willing to perform his family duty and marry Ruth, whose Jewish husband had died in Moab. Ruth's behavior had been honorable, and she had done what she could to let Boaz know she was willing to be his wife, but now she could do nothing except to sit still and wait.

Christians need to remember this lesson today. All too often we rush ahead of the Lord, fearful that things won't work out unless we take matters into our own hands. When the Jews were being invaded by the Assyrian armies and felt they needed an alliance with Pharaoh, God warned, "The Egyptians shall help in vain, and to no purpose: therefore have I cried concerning this, their strength is to sit still…In returning and rest shall ye be saved; in quietness and in confidence shall be your strength."

He exhorts us, "Be still, and know that I am God."

Scripture:
Ruth 3:18; Isaiah 30:7-15; Psalm 46:10

The God Who Provides

Now the God of hope fill you with
all joy and peace in believing.

There are seven beautiful titles ascribed to God in the New Testament.

The God of love. First of all, we need love, and "God is love."

The God of all grace. God saves us by His grace because "the God of all grace...hath called us unto his eternal glory."

The God of peace. He satisfies the need for peace in the believer's soul, and He is called "the God of peace" five times in the New Testament.

The God of all comfort. Our God is called "the Father of mercies, and the God of all comfort" because He "comforteth us in all our tribulation," thus enabling us also to provide comfort to others "by the comfort wherewith we ourselves are comforted of God."

The God of patience. We do "have need of patience."

The God of glory. It was "the God of glory" who first called Abraham.

The God of hope. By His Spirit He fills us with joy and peace, with power and abundant hope, blessing us "with all spiritual blessings...in Christ."

Scripture:

Romans 15:13,33; 1 John 4:8; 1 Peter 5:8; 2 Corinthians 1:3-4;
Hebrews 10:36; Acts 7:2; Ephesians 1:3

Thanks for Everything

*…giving thanks always for all things unto God and
the Father in the name of our Lord Jesus Christ.*

Being thankful for everything is one of the evidences that a Christian is indeed "filled with the Spirit."

And not only *for* everything, but *in* everything as well. "In every thing give thanks: for this is the will of God in Christ Jesus concerning you."

These two commands are easy to obey when the living is easy, as the song says, though we might easily forget to do so. But when the Lord is allowing us to hurt for a while, thanksgiving becomes hard. It is hard while we are experiencing the difficulty and just as hard when it has passed with no relief in sight. The two small prepositions "in" and "for" are different in New Testament Greek as well as in modern English, and God really wants us to learn how to thank Him both during and after the hard experience.

James, the Lord's brother, urges us, "Count it all joy when ye fall into divers temptations [or various testings]; knowing this, that the trying of your faith worketh patience. But let patience have her perfect work, that ye may be perfect and entire, wanting nothing."

Scripture:
Ephesians 5:18-20; 1 Thessalonians 5:18; James 1:2-3

Even as Others

*[You] were by nature the children
of wrath, even as others.*

There are seven significant similes in Ephesians that employ the pungent connecting phrase "even as." The first is our text, comparing our past life to that of the ungodly world around us. The second speaks of the unity of our calling in Christ. "There is one body, and one Spirit, even as ye are called in one hope of your calling."

The next simile tells of the forgiveness received when we begin a transformed life. "Be ye kind one to another, tender-hearted, forgiving one another, even as God for Christ's sake hath forgiven you."

The last four all speak of the beautiful analogy of the love of husbands and wives to the love of Christ for His church. "For the husband is the head of the wife, even as Christ is the head of the church: and he is the savior of the body." "Husbands, love your wives, even as Christ also loved the church, and gave himself for it." "For no man ever yet hated his own flesh; but nourisheth and cherisheth it, even as the Lord the church." "Nevertheless let every one of you in particular so love his wife even as himself."

Scripture:
Ephesians 2:3; 4:4,32; 5:23-33

"I Will" Versus "I Will"

How art thou fallen from heaven, O Lucifer, son of the morning! how art thou cut down to the ground.

Lucifer" means "light-bearer." The name occurs only here, but there is no doubt as to who is in view. "And the great dragon was cast out, that old serpent, called the Devil."

Why was he cast out? "For thou hast said in thine heart, I will ascend into heaven, I will exalt my throne above the stars of God: I will sit also upon the mount of the congregation, in the sides of the north: I will ascend above the heights of the clouds; I will be like the Most High."

The ability to say "I will" or "I will not" is one of the prerogatives that God has instilled into His creatures. Obviously, Lucifer's "I will" is in direct opposition to God's will.

The first time God said "I will" in the Bible, He promised Adam a help meet for him: "I will make him an help meet for him." And then He spoke directly to the serpent: "I will put enmity between thee and the woman, and between thy seed and her seed."

The two I wills are joined in conflict and have been until this day.

Scripture:

Isaiah 14:12-14; Revelation 12:9; Genesis 2:18; 3:15

Now and Then

Now we see through a glass, darkly;
but then face to face.

There is a great contrast between now and then. We see only dimly now, but at least we see! We only know partially, but we do know! What we shall see and know in the future is already ours, but only in hope and promise. "For what a man seeth, why doth he yet hope for?"

The Christian life knows many such paradoxes. We now "are the sons of God," and yet we are "waiting for the adoption." Right now in Christ, "we have redemption through his blood," but the Holy Spirit is "the earnest of our inheritance until the redemption of the purchased possession."

We only have "the firstfruits of the Spirit" while we are awaiting "the redemption of our body," but by "the Holy Spirit of God" we "are sealed unto the day of redemption," and therefore we already possess "redemption through his blood, even the forgiveness of sins."

Similarly, the Father already "hath translated us into the kingdom of his dear Son," but "we must through much tribulation enter into the kingdom of God."

Scripture:

1 Corinthians 13:12-13; Romans 8:23-24;
Ephesians 1:7,14; 4:30; Colossians 1:14; Acts 14:22

Life Below the Surface

Search me, O God, and know my heart:
try me, and know my thoughts.

Very seldom do we bother to look at life below the surface. In our daily addiction to activity, we rarely take the time to plunge beneath the mundane and the ordinary and the obvious. Various reasons exist for our refusal to see what lies beneath what we know as normal. In a sense, looking past the obvious is vital if we want to honestly understand how everything is made and why it works the way it does. And sometimes we need help to do so, to help us discern what we find when we peer through the microscope. Not looking through the lens, however, ultimately leads to uncertainty.

Examinations, both physical and spiritual, are therefore both necessary and therapeutic. All of the hidden recesses must be searched, for only in doing so can we begin to deal with life as God has made it. Of course, our Creator is the One who can perfectly see below the surface, for He made it all. Scientists can peer through the lenses of powerful microscopes to understand the smallest components of the life God designed, but only the Creator can give us answers, as He has done in His Word.

Scripture:
Psalm 139:23-24

SIGN UP FOR ICR's FREE PUBLICATIONS!

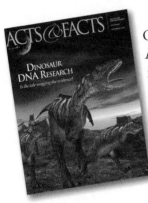

VISIT ICR ONLINE

ICR.org offers a wealth of resources and information on creation and biblical worldview issues.

✓ Read our daily news postings on today's hottest science topics
✓ Explore the Evidence for Creation
✓ Investigate our graduate and professional education programs
✓ Dive into our archive of 40 years of scientific articles

✓ Listen to current and past radio programs
✓ Watch our *That's a Fact* video show
✓ Visit our *Science Essentials* education blog
✓ And more!

Visit our Online Store at www.icr.org/store
for more great resources.

INSTITUTE
for CREATION
RESEARCH

P. O. Box 59029
Dallas, TX 75229
800.337.0375